I0390494

Essex Ontario in Colour Photos, Saving Our History One Photo at a Time

Photography
by Barbara Raué
2015

Series Name:
Cruising Ontario

Book 122: Essex

Cover photo: 122 Talbot Street South

Series Name: Cruising Ontario
Saving Our History One Photo at a Time
in colour photos

Books Available in Alphabetical Order:
Aberfoyle, Acton, Alton, Ancaster, Arthur, Aylmer, Ayr, Bloomingdale, Brantford, Burlington, Caledon, Caledonia, Cambridge, Clifford, Conestogo, Delhi, Dorchester to Aylmer, Drayton, Drumbo, Dundas, Eden Mills, Elmira, Elora, Fergus, Guelph, Hagersville, Hamilton, Hanover, Harriston, Hespeler, Jarvis, Kitchener, Linwood, Listowel, London, Lucknow, Mono, Mount Forest, Neustadt, New Hamburg, Niagara-on-the-Lake, Oakville, Orangeville, Orillia, Owen Sound, Palmerston, Peterborough, Port Elgin, Preston, Rockwood, Seaforth, Sheffield, Shelburne, Simcoe, Southampton, St. Jacobs, St. Thomas, Stoney Creek, Stratford, Tillsonburg, Waterdown, Waterrford, Waterloo, Wellesley, Wingham

Other Books by Barbara Raue

Coins of Gold

Arrows, Indians and Love

The Life and Times of Barbara
Volume 1: Inventions That Have Enhanced My Life
Volume 2: Entertainment That I Have Enjoyed
Volume 3: East Coast Trips
Volume 4: Olympics Have Always Intrigued Me
Volume 5: Wonders of the World
Volume 6: Caribbean Cruises We Have Enjoyed
Volume 7: Animals
Volume 8: Storms and Other Major Disasters in My Lifetime
Volume 9: Wars, Terrorist Attacks and Major Disasters

The Cromwell Family Book

Laura Secord Discovered

Daddy Where Are You?

Visit Barbara's website to view all of her books
http://barbararaue.ca

Amherstburg and Sandwich, the first towns to be established in Essex County, were first settled in 1796 after the British evacuated Fort Detroit. The populations of both towns were augmented by people immigrating from the United States to the south after the American Revolutionary War (1775-1783), especially from the City of Detroit by those who chose to remain British subjects, people known as "United Empire Loyalists".

After the American Revolution and the War of 1812 (1812-1815), people continued to migrate north to the area, and came from the east from Lake Ontario and the St. Lawrence River of Lower Canada seeking land. Settlers began to move eastward along the north shore of Lake Erie. Land was purchased from the Indians in the southern half of the current county. The British Court made land available for settlement provided that certain improvements were made to the land within a year and that it was not used for speculation. This area became known as the "New Settlement" (as compared to the "Old Settlement" of the towns of Amherstburg and Sandwich). Settlers in the area included Hessians who fought for the British against the American rebels, and Pennsylvania Dutch (Mennonites).

In 1854 the Great Western Railway connected the Detroit frontier with the east, crossing Essex County. The Canadian terminal was in Windsor, which consequently forged ahead of the other towns of the county. Other railway lines were built that connected settlements in Kingsville, Harrow, Essex and Leamington.

By the late 19th century Essex County had seen fur trading and logging, land clearing and farming, road building and railway development, saw mills and gristmills, railway stations and water ports. By this time the forests were disappearing, replaced by fertile farmland.

Essex is a town in Essex County in southwestern Ontario with its municipal borders extending to Lake Erie. The Talbot Trail attributed to the growth of Essex in the last half of the 19th century.

Essex was one of the first counties to be settled in Upper Canada mostly by French people in the mid-18th century. Around 1749, the first permanent settlements began to appear on what is now the Canadian side of the Detroit River which despite its name is a strait connecting Lake Huron and the smaller Lake Saint Clair in the north and to Lake Erie in the south, as part of the Great Lakes system.

Essex County is largely composed of clay-based soils, with sandy soils along the beaches and shores. For the most part, Essex County is flat farmland, with some woodlots. When farmers first arrived, they encountered difficulty in trying to clear the extremely thick forests that covered Essex County. The farmers starved the trees from nourishment by cutting deep gashes in the bark, and burned them to clear the way to get to the fertile soils underneath. The fires were so intense that the reddish glow could be seen from Fort Chicago, 300 miles away, as millions of cords of wood burned.

On August 10, 1907, at the Essex Station there was a large explosion that sent shockwaves across the county and into some parts of nearby Michigan. A train cart containing 5000 pounds of nitroglycerine ignited. The blast sent debris over 600 yards away, killed two people and injured many more. The boom of the explosion caused plaster to fall from the ceilings of buildings in Windsor and windows to rattle as far as Detroit. The Essex Station was very heavily damaged. The Essex Station was rebuilt to its previous form and remains a recognizable landmark in the town.

Table of Contents

The gift of this mural to the town of Essex to celebrate Essex Rotary's 70th birthday is a visual history of the men and women who have committed themselves to improve the lives and community of their fellow man. It depicts many of the club's international, community, club and vocational ventures.

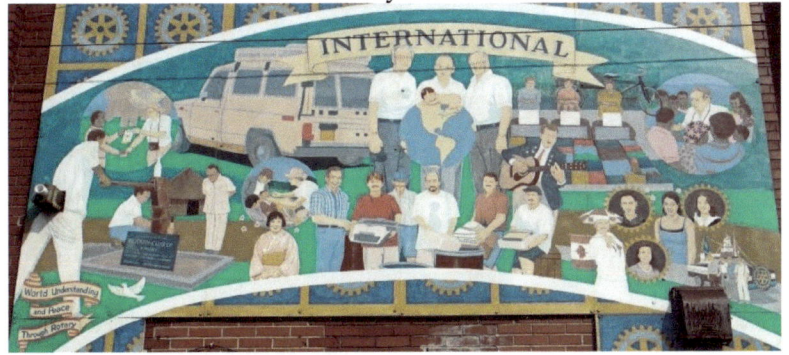

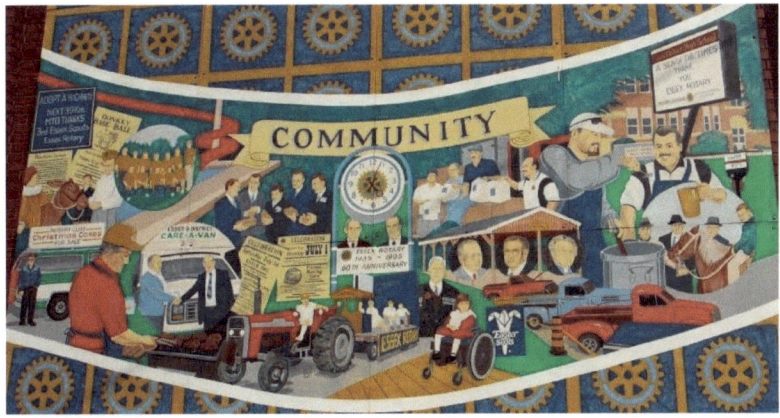

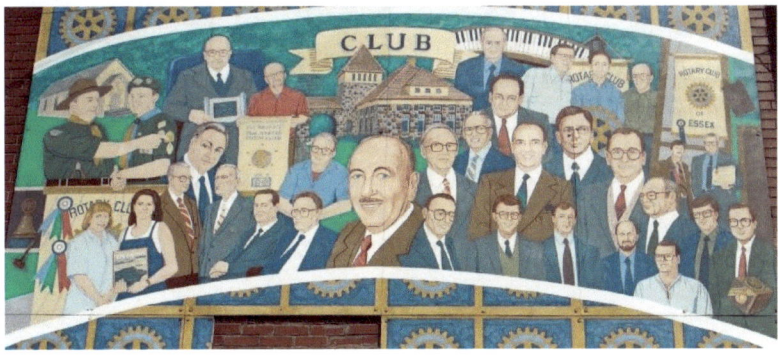

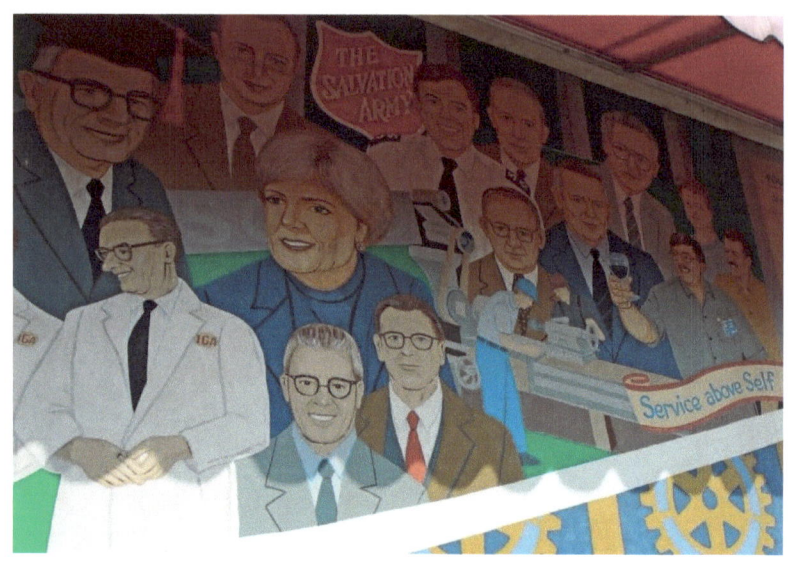

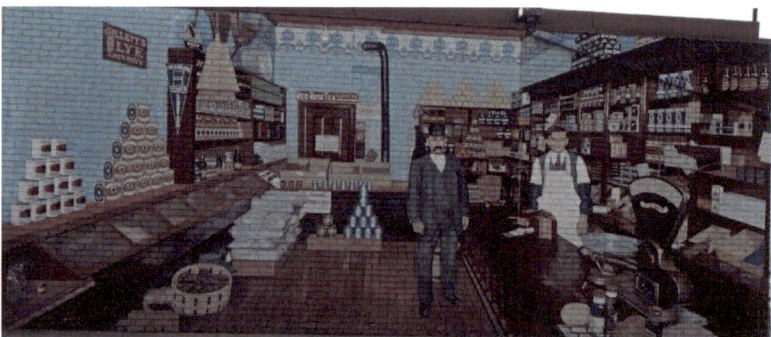

The interior of A. Raines' store was typical of the six grocery stores in Essex, circa 1910, when the population was 1700 and electric power was supplied by Naylor Lumber Mill.

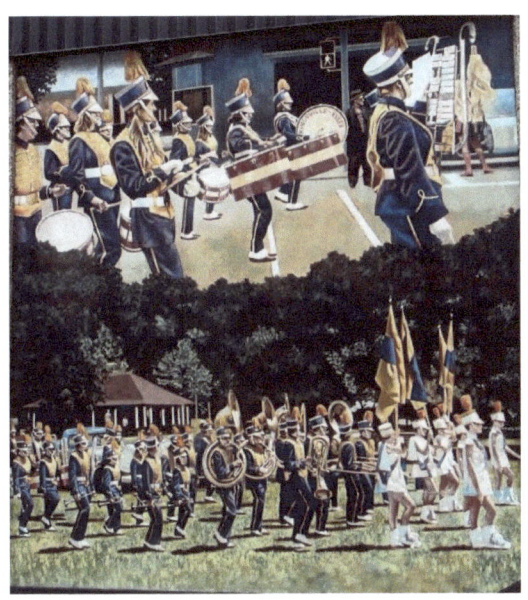

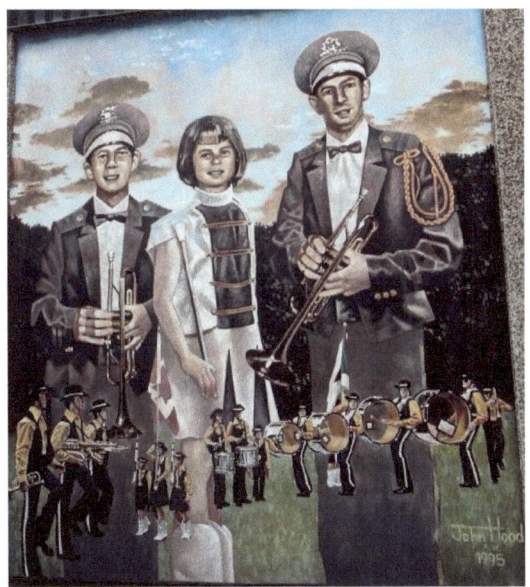

The Kingsville Essex Associated Band is the longest continuously operating community band in Ontario.

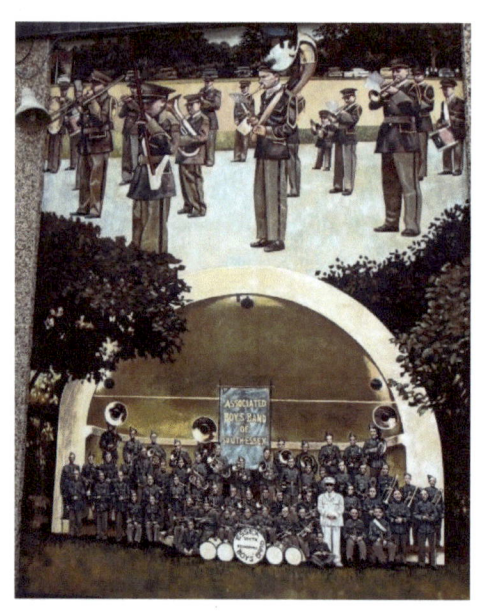

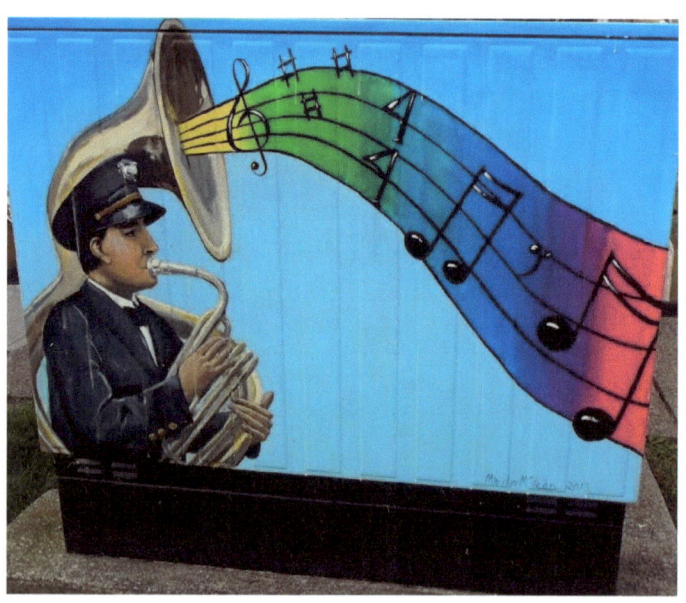

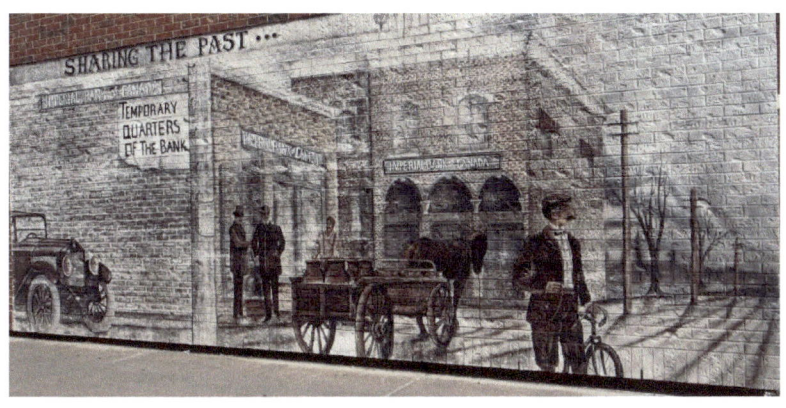

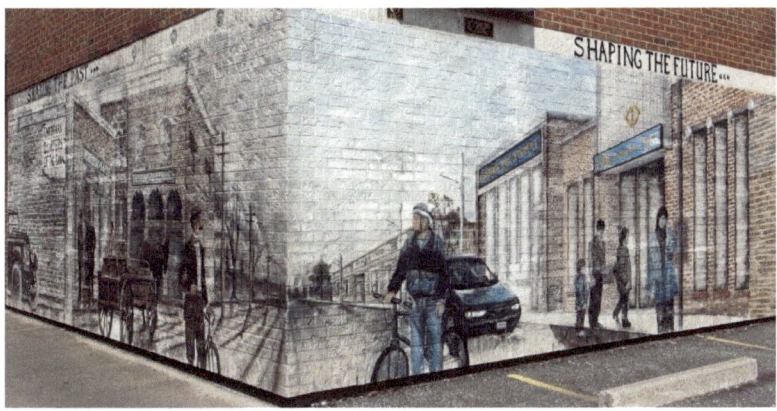

Sharing the Past …Shaping the Future mural

Since 1885 The Canadian Imperial Bank of Commerce and its employees have been helping citizens of Essex and surrounding area build a strong healthy community helping people fulfil their dreams.

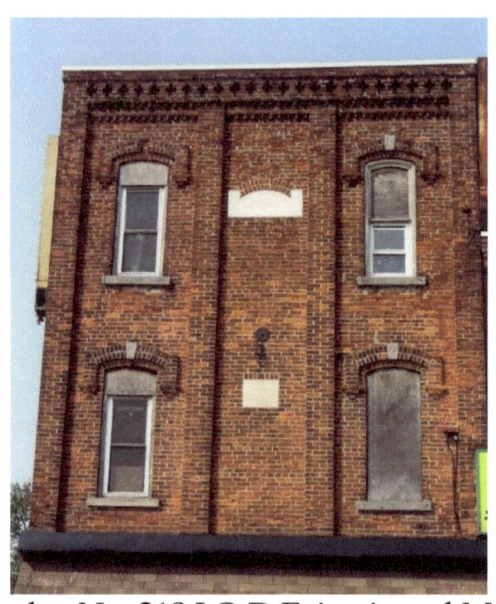

Enterprise Lodge No. 218 I.O.D.E. instituted March 18, 1879
Cornice, dentil moulding, pilasters, keystones and voussoirs

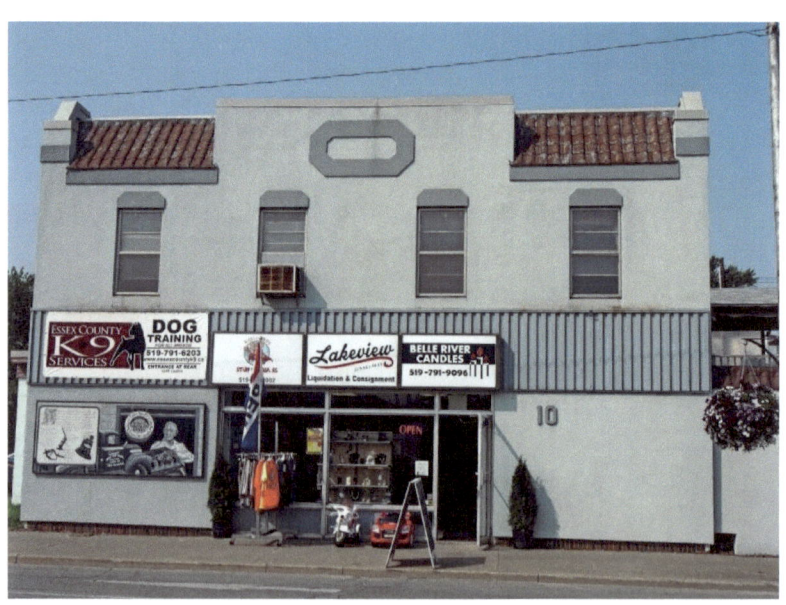

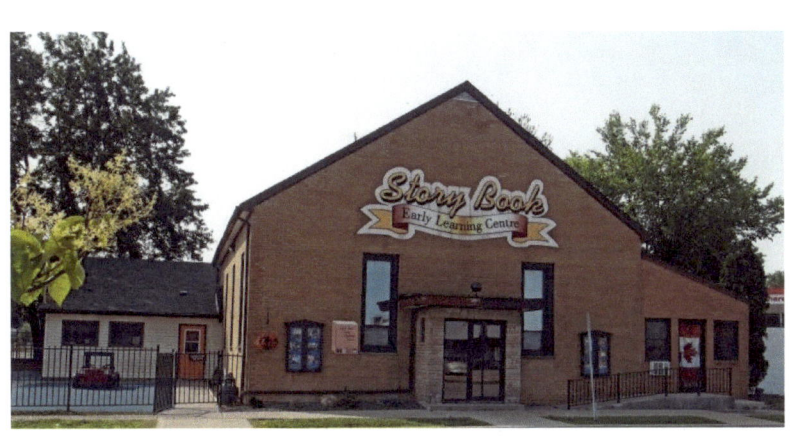

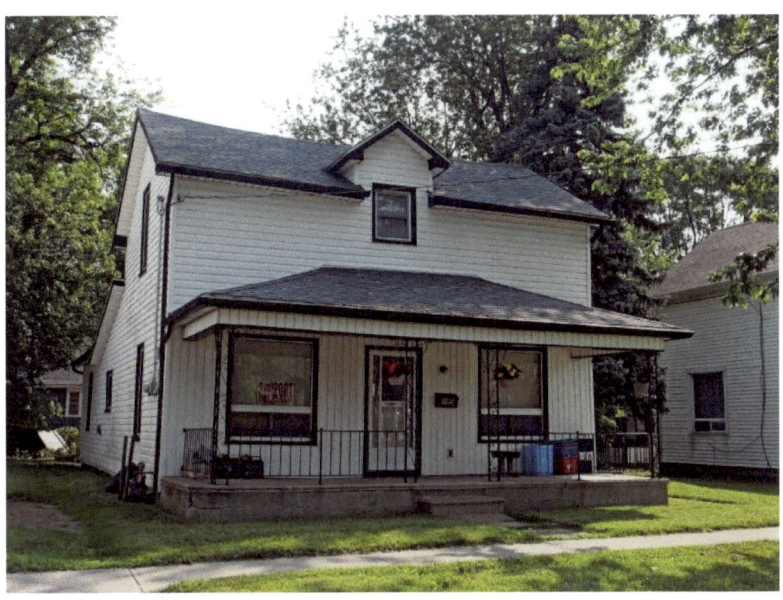

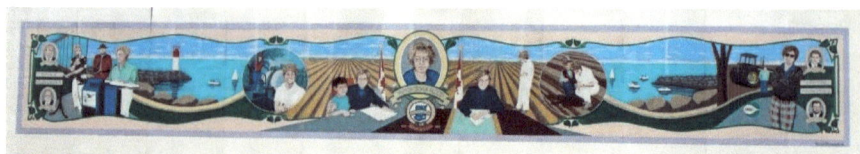

The new Municipality of Essex came into being on January 1, 1999 with Joan Flood as its first mayor (centre picture). Also shown are mayors of the four founding municipalities: Carl Davison of Colchester North, Paul Innes of Colchester South. Peter Timmins of Harrow, and Vic McMurren of Essex. The new town of Essex is a productive agricultural area, has two active commercial areas (the old towns of Essex and Harrow), and a picturesque waterfront.

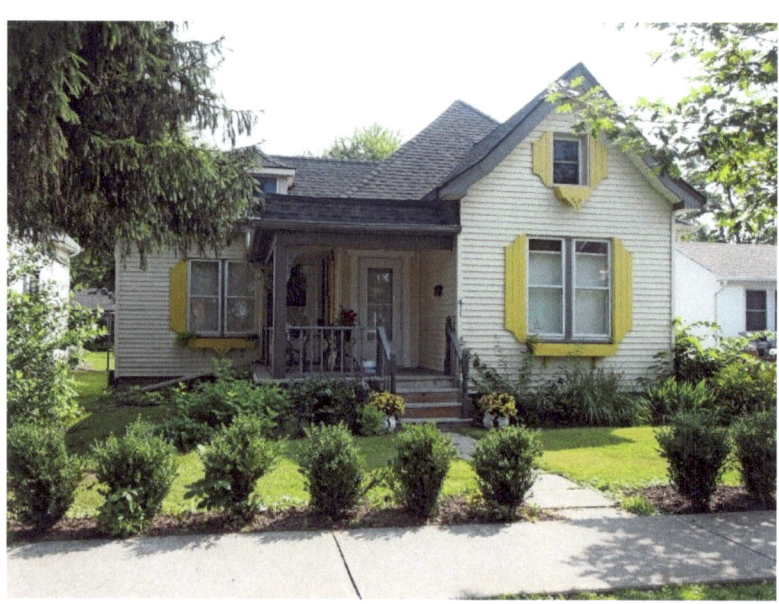

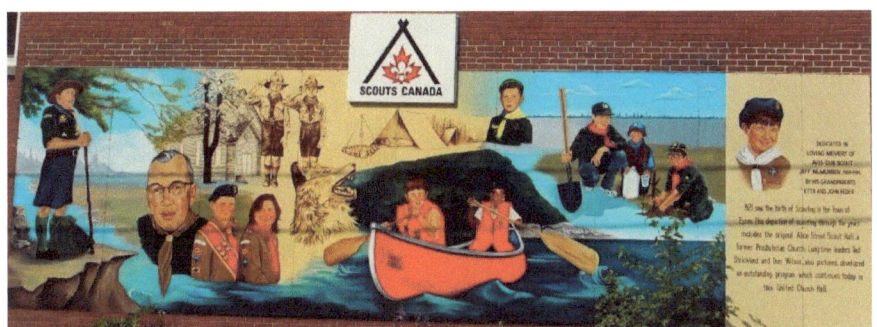

Boy Scouts mural

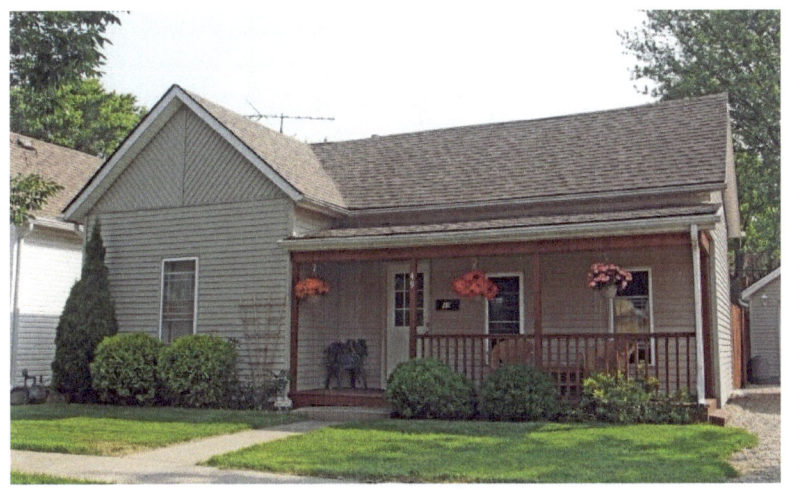

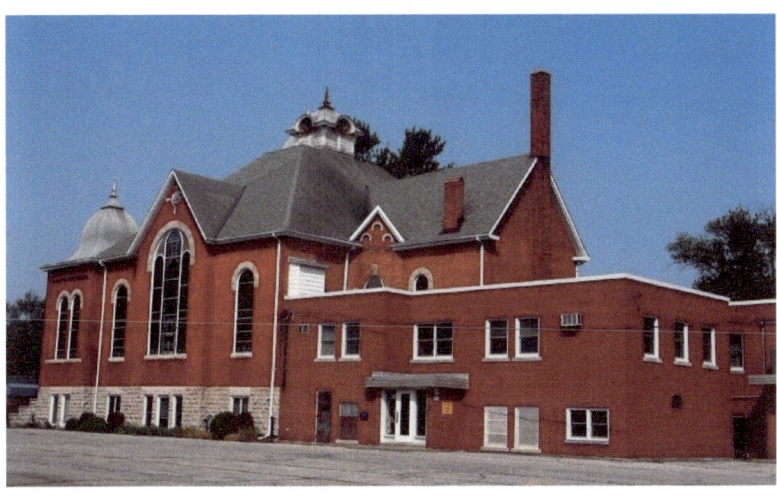

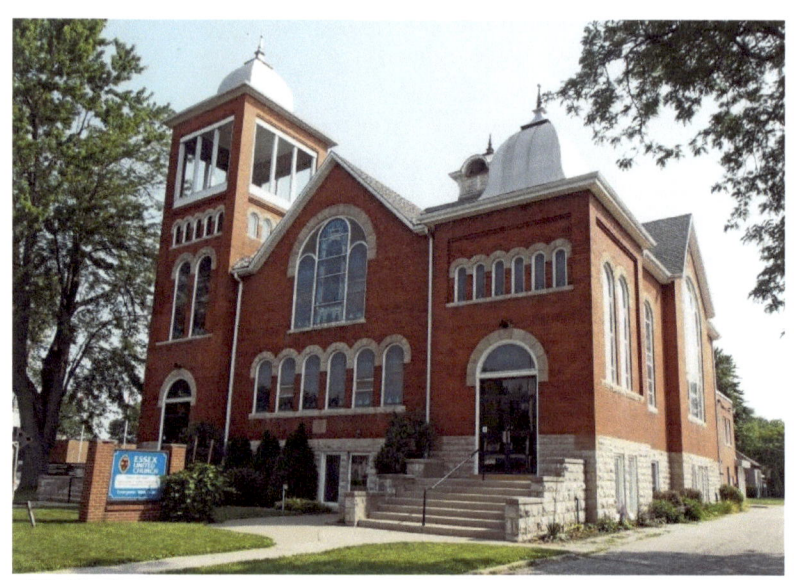

53 Talbot Street South - Essex United Church (Grace Methodist Church) – 1908

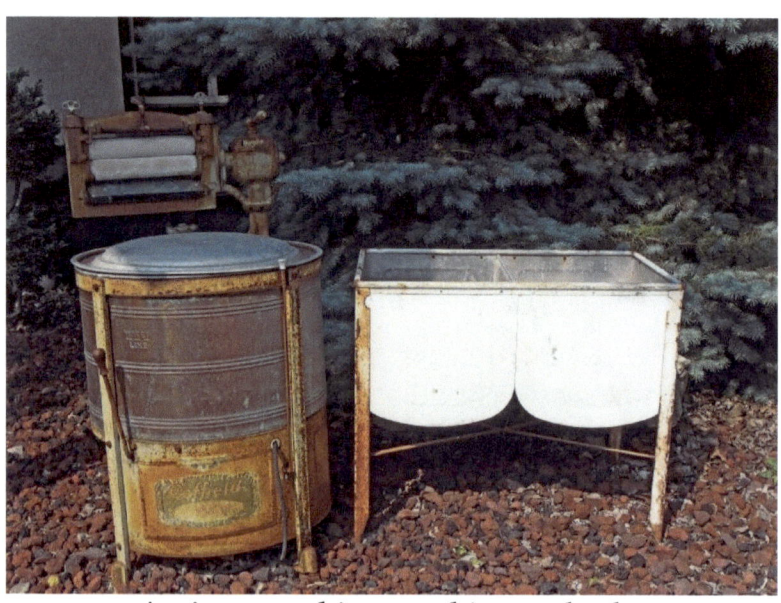

Antique washing machine and tubs

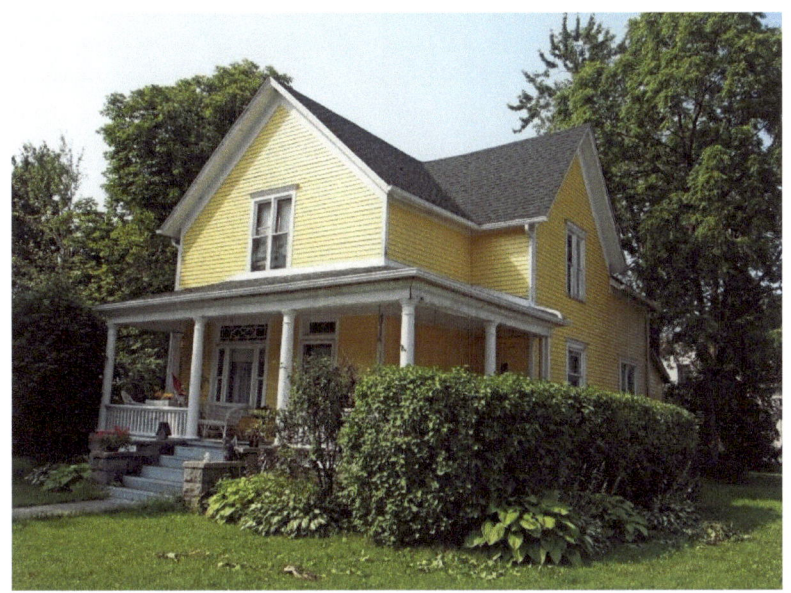

Talbot Street South - Gothic

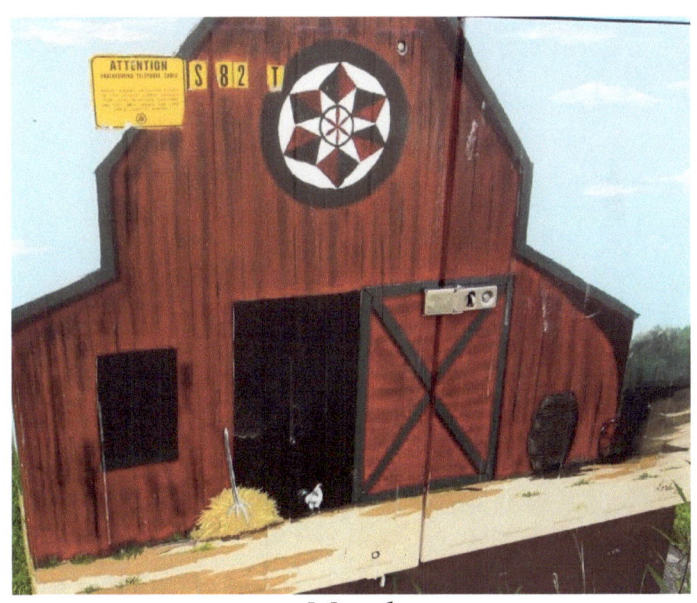

Mural

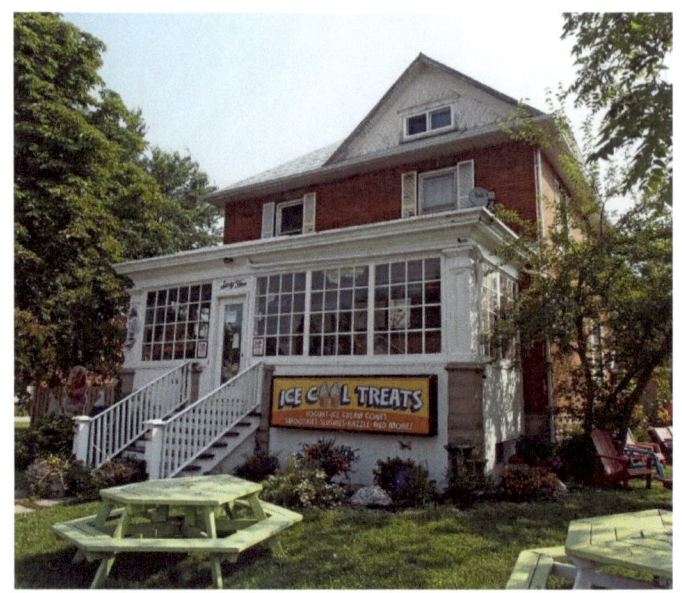

65 Talbot Street South

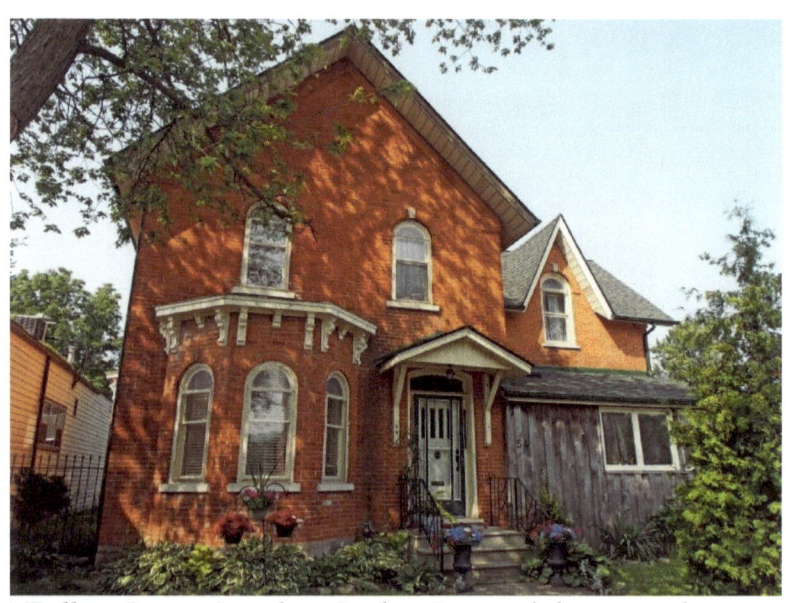

54 Talbot Street South – Gothic Revival, bay window with cornice brackets

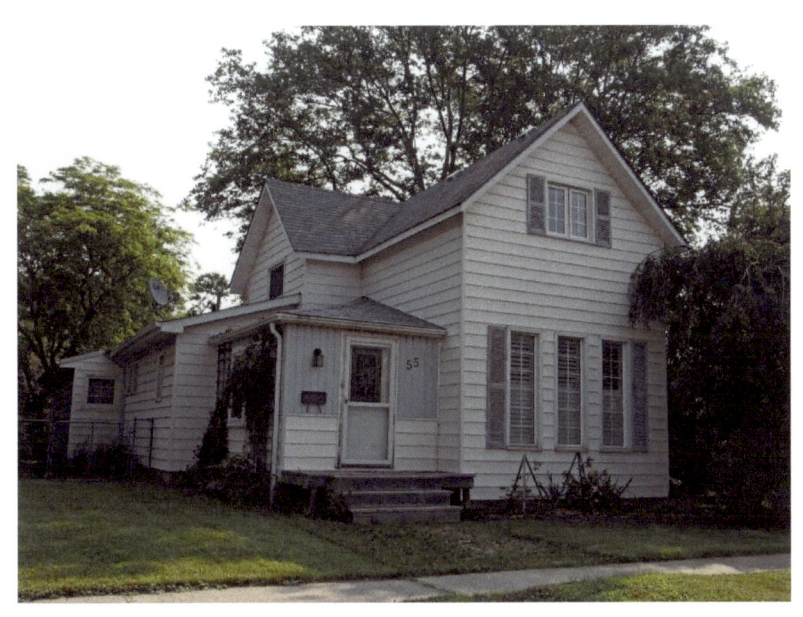

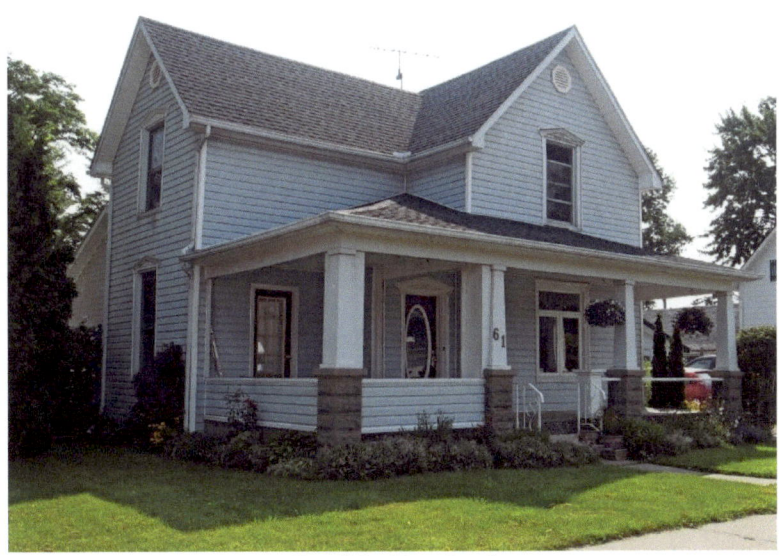

Gothic Revival

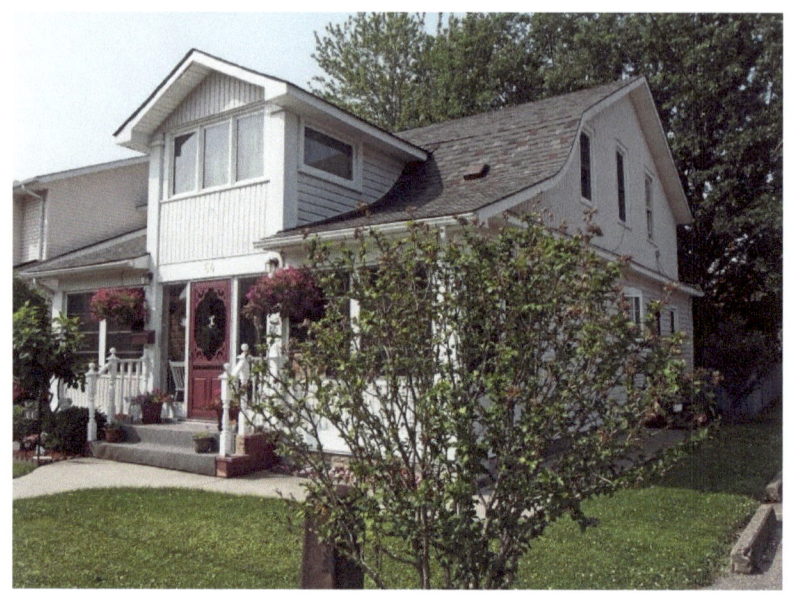

Irwin Avenue – Cape Dutch architecture, large dormer

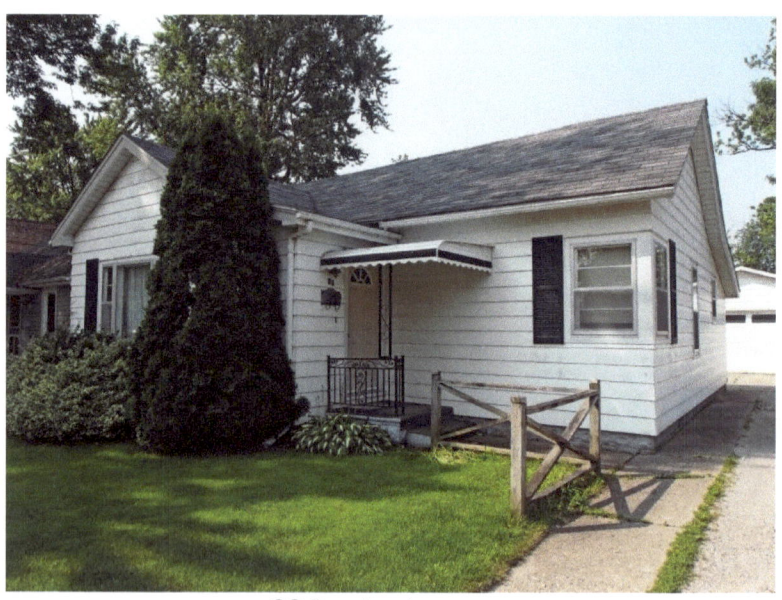

90 Irwin Avenue

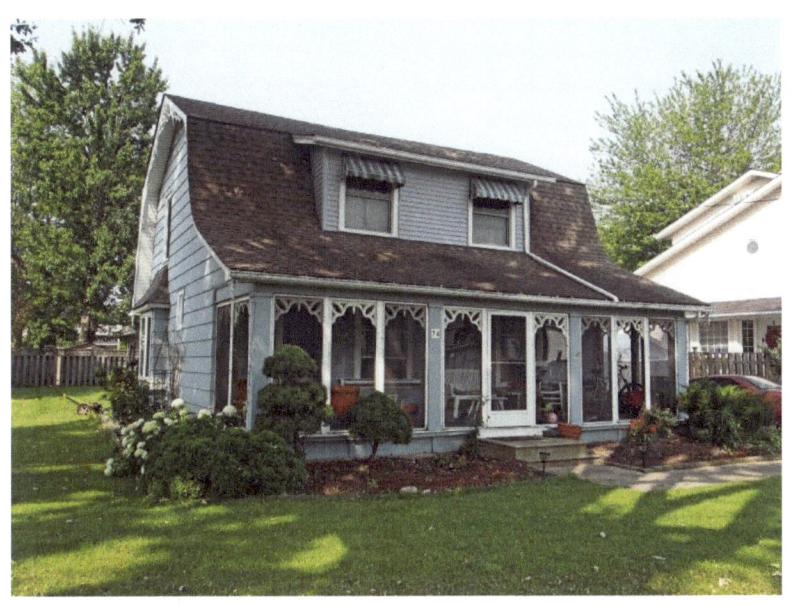

74 Irwin Avenue – Cape Dutch architecture

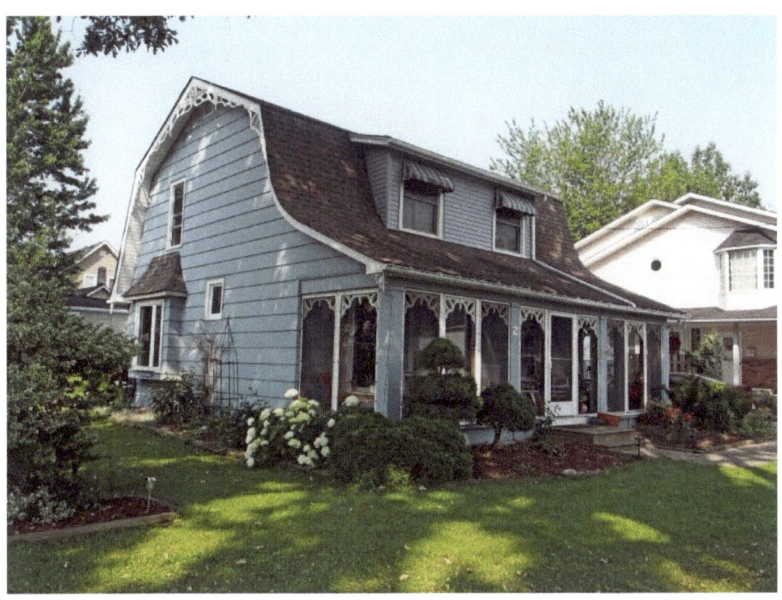

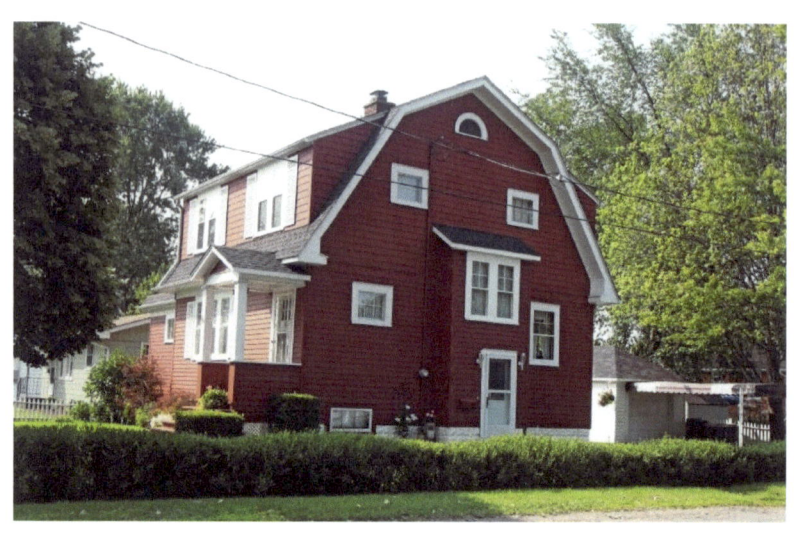

80 Irwin Avenue – Dutch Colonial style

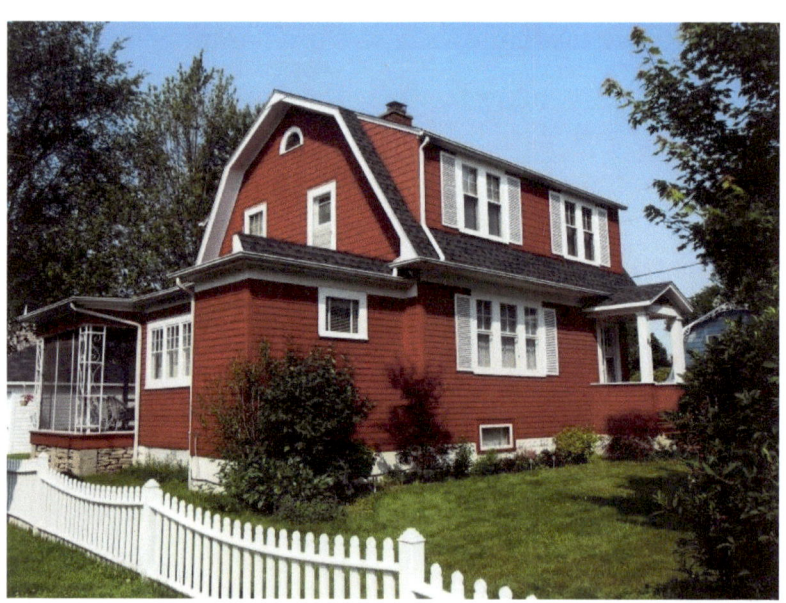

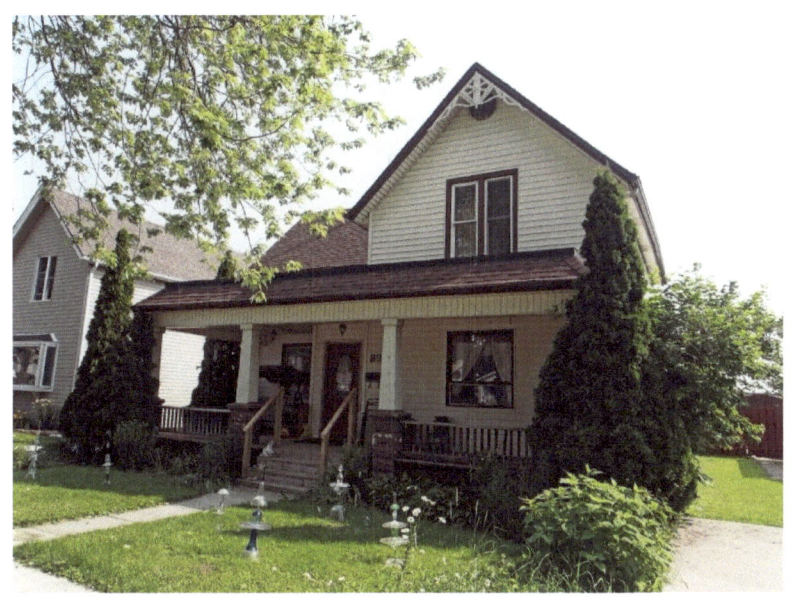

89 Irwin Avenue – Gothic Revival

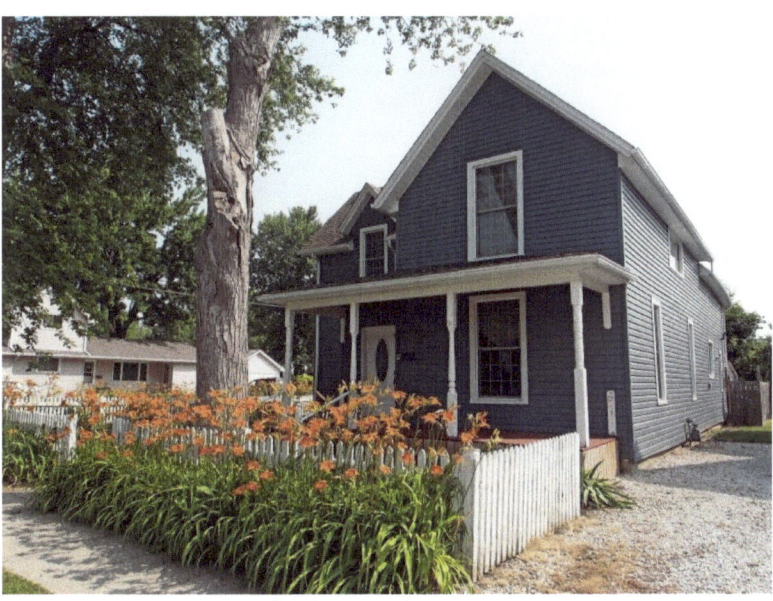

81 Irwin Avenue

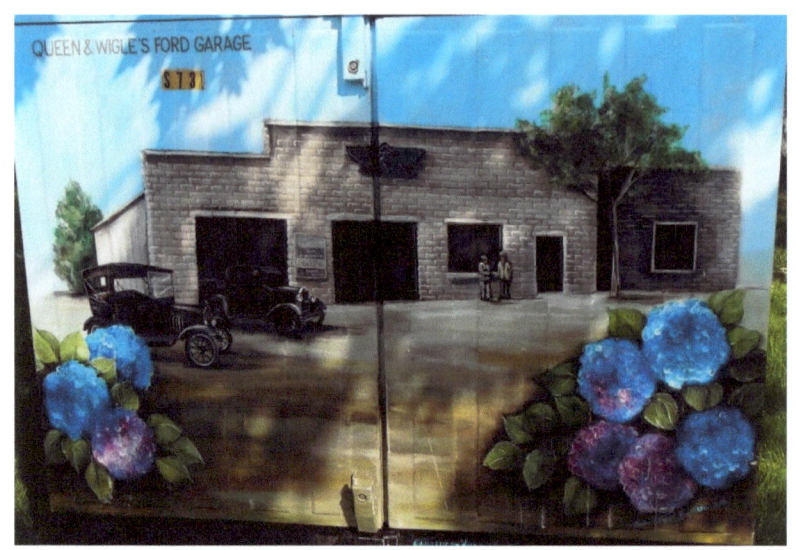

Mural of Queen and Wigle's Ford Garage

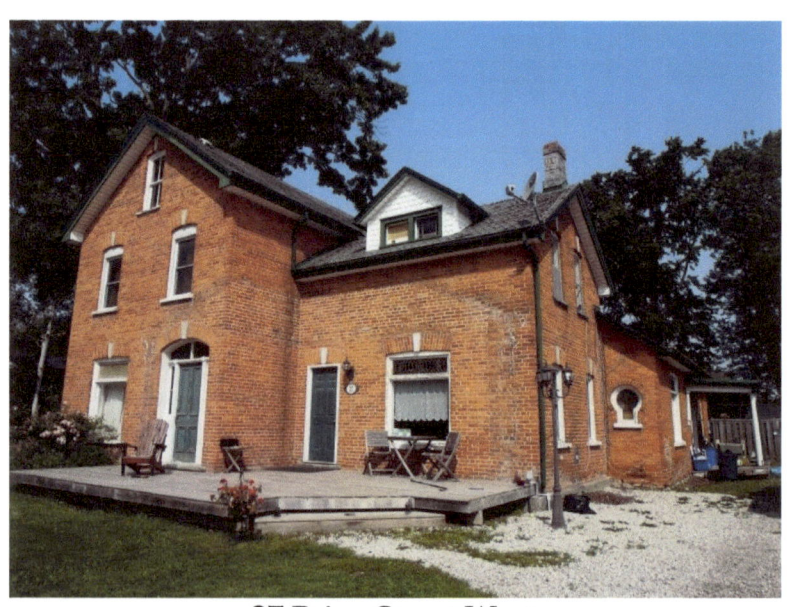

27 Brien Street West

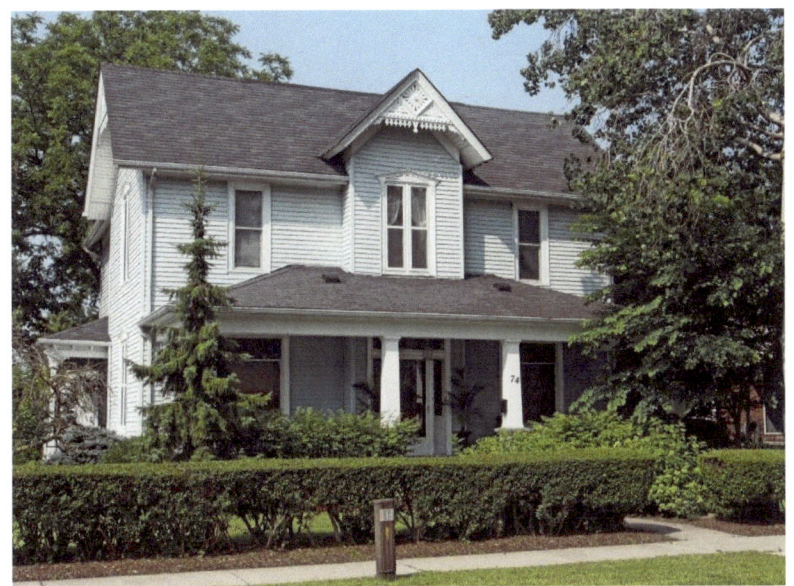

74 Alice Street

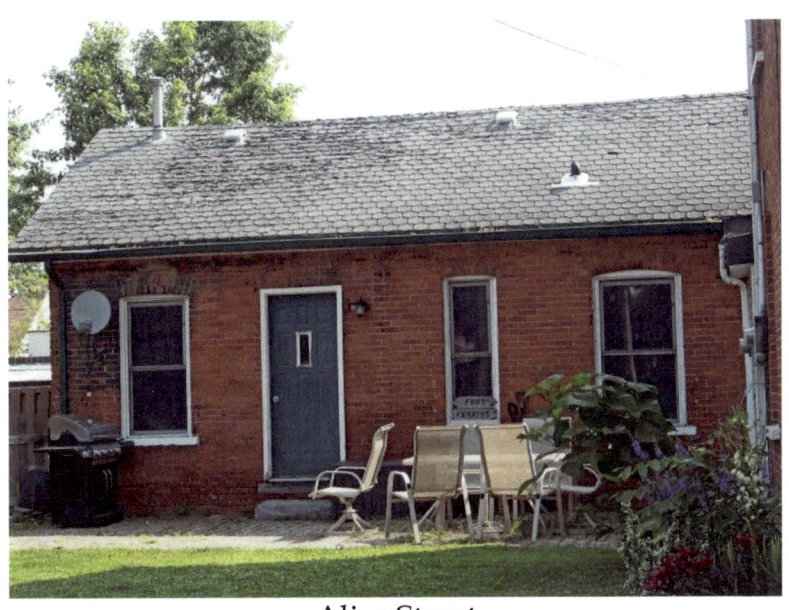

Alice Street

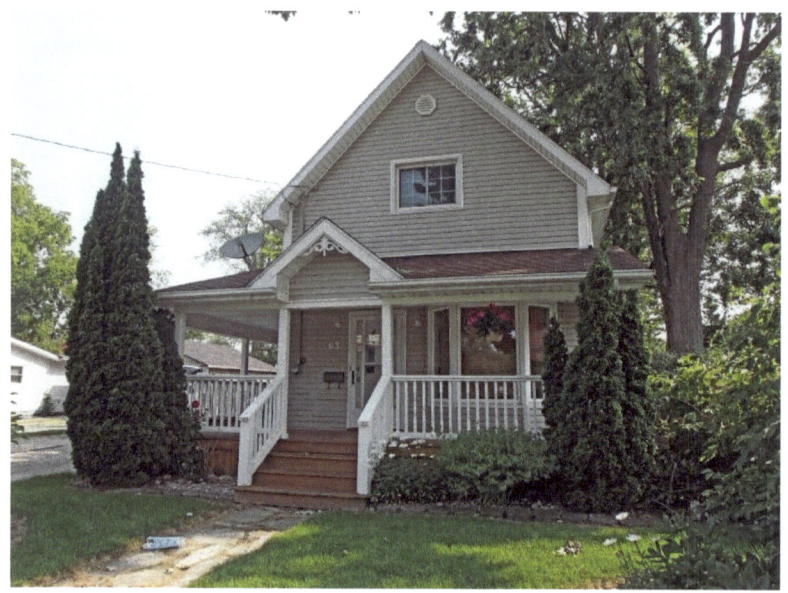

63 Alice Street

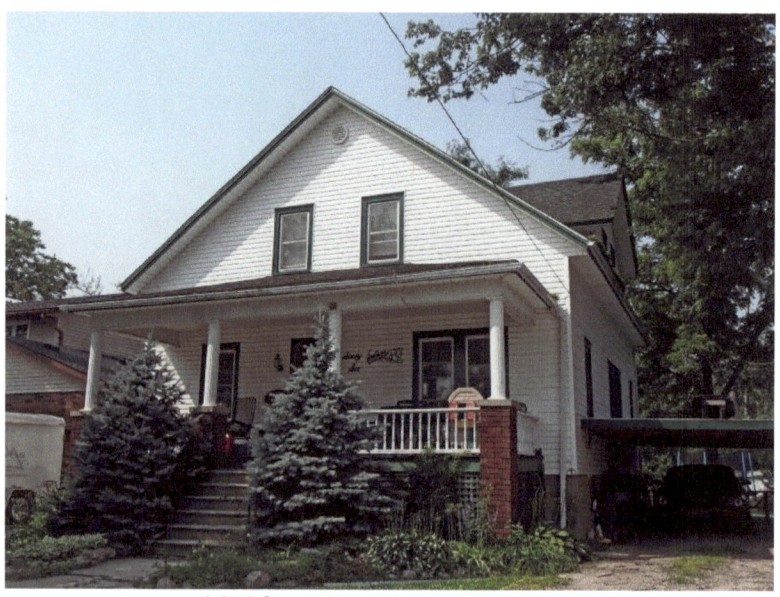

66 Alice Street - vernacular

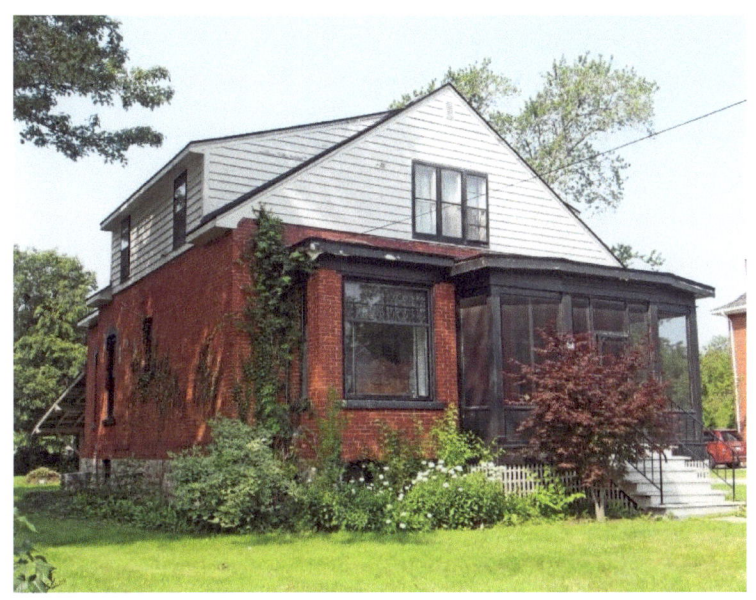

62 Alice Street - vernacular

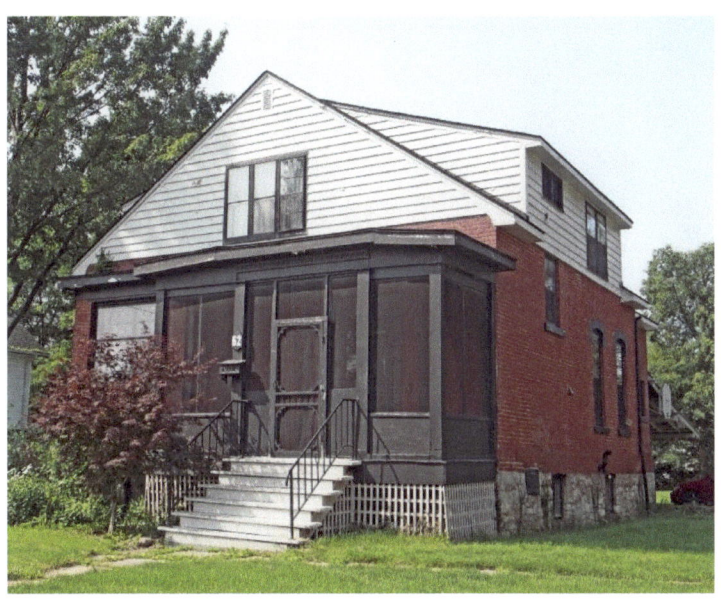

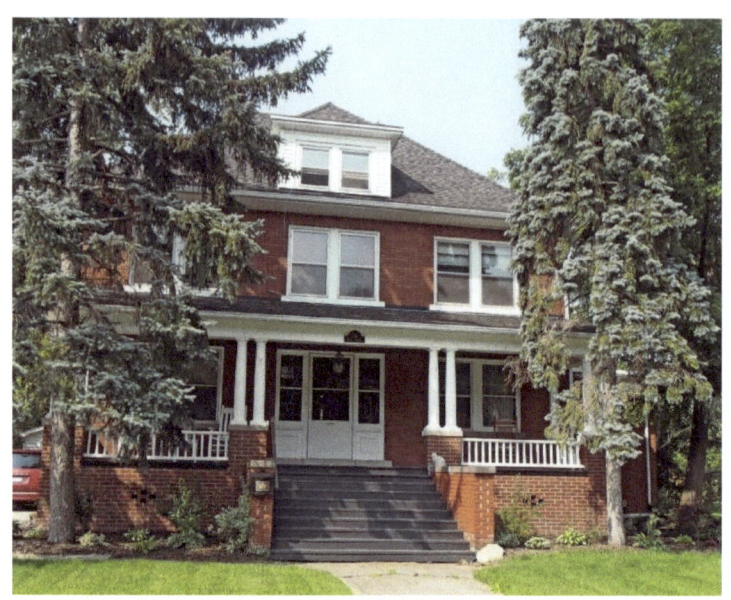

54 Alice Street – Italianate, hipped roof, dormer,
Doric columns

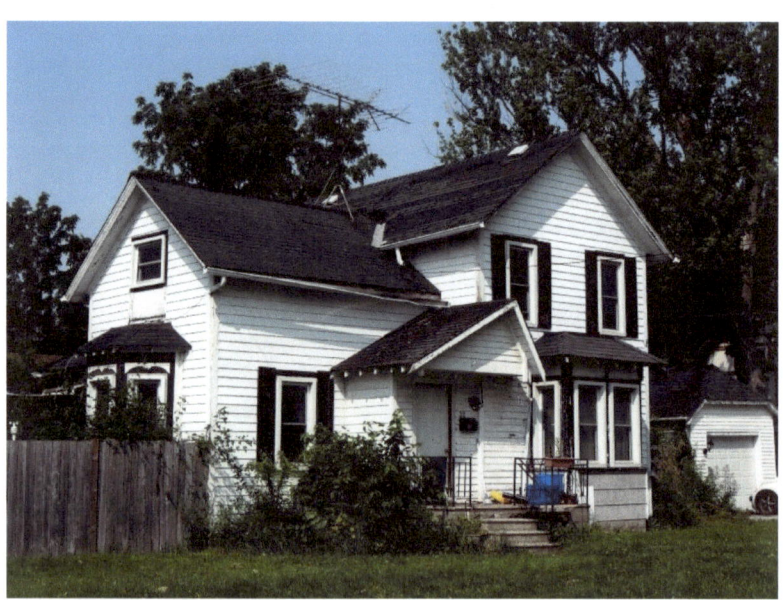

32 Alice Street - Gothic

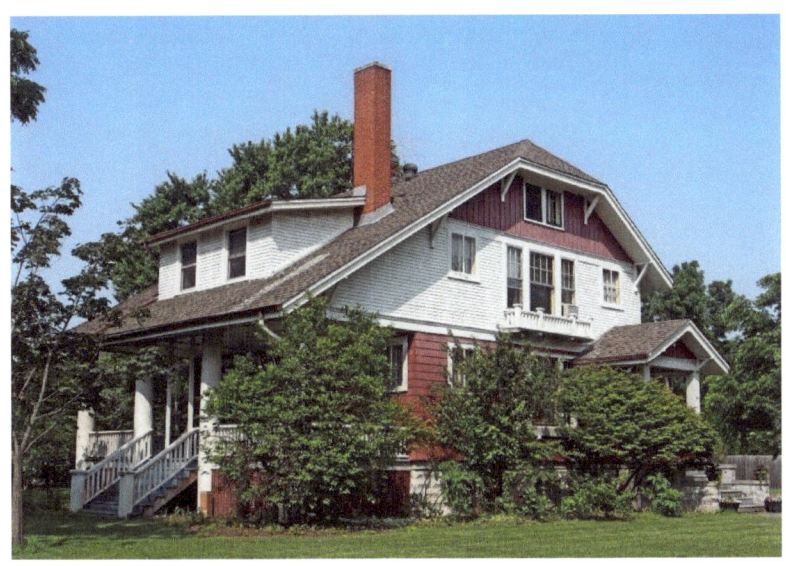

46 Alice Street - vernacular

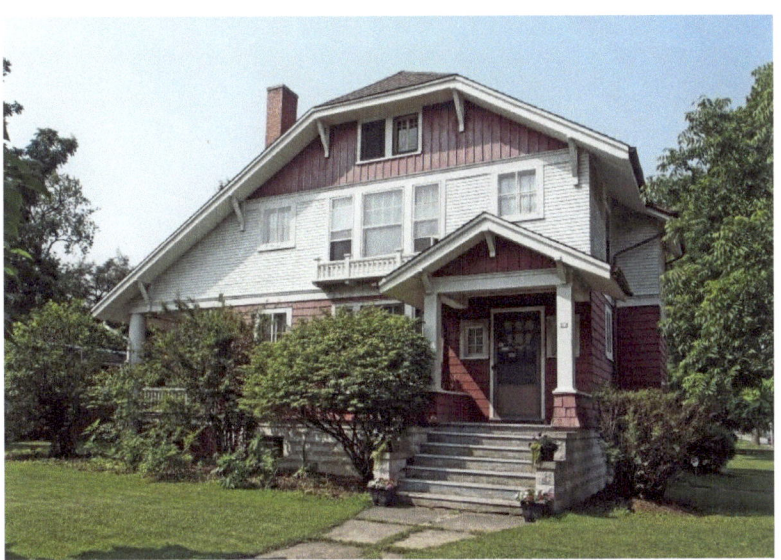

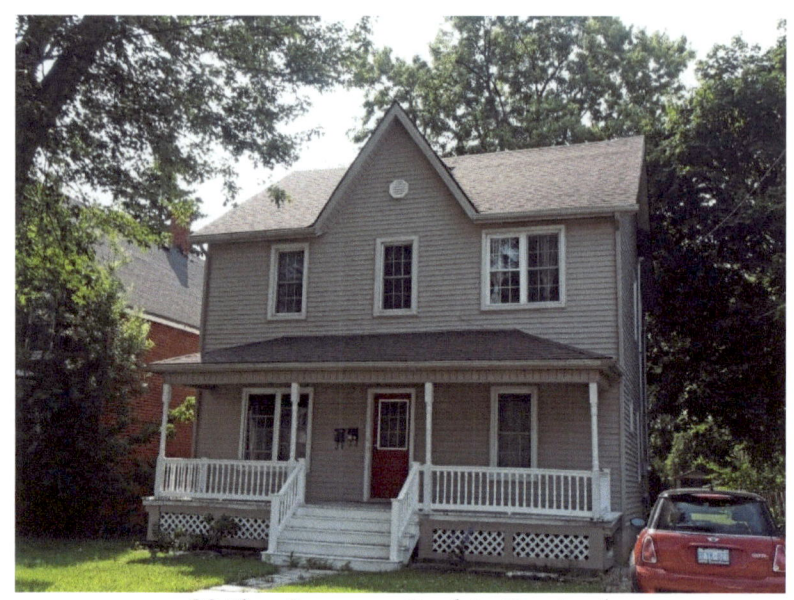

22 Iler Street – Gothic Revival

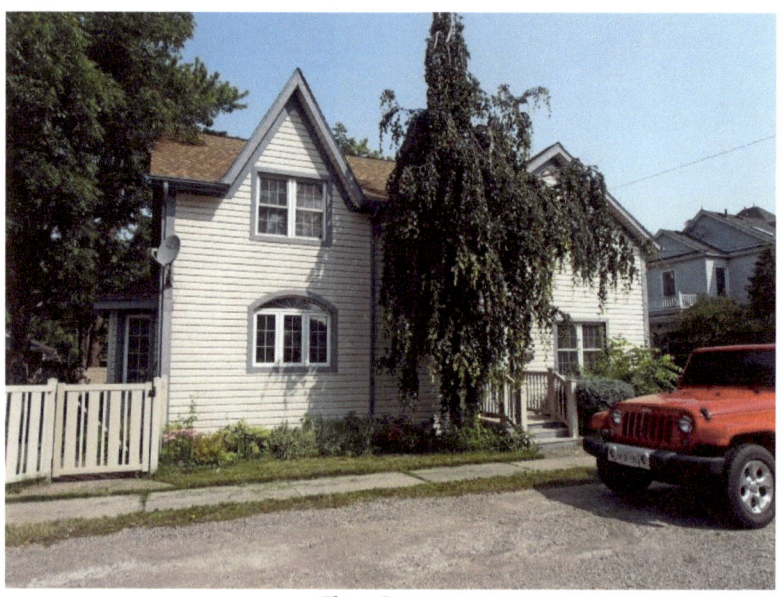

Iler Street

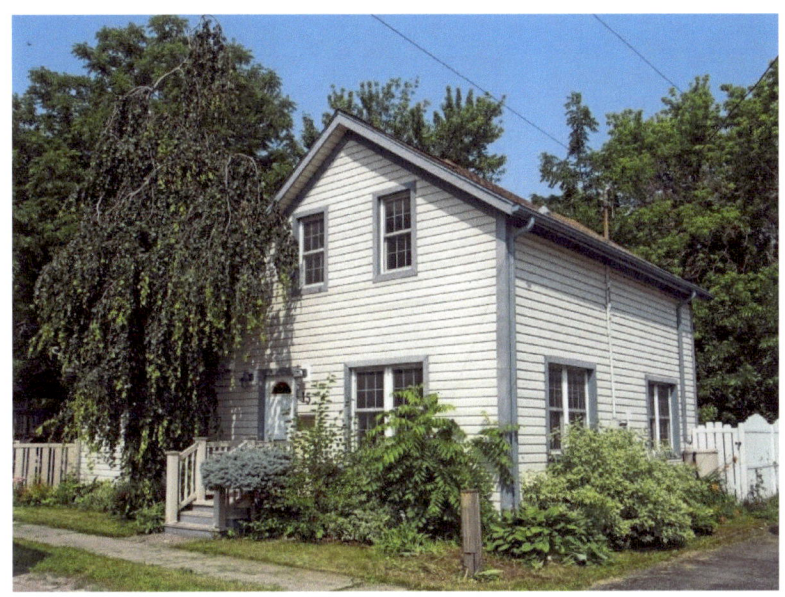

15 Iler Street

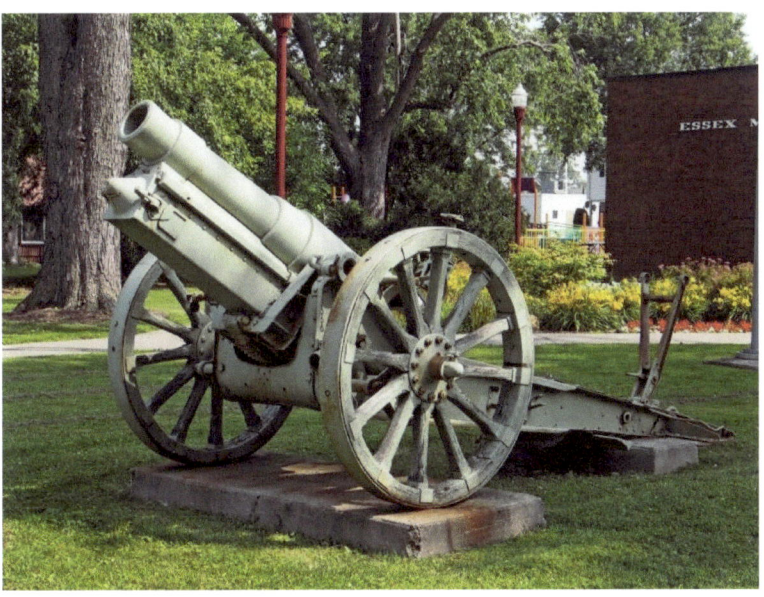

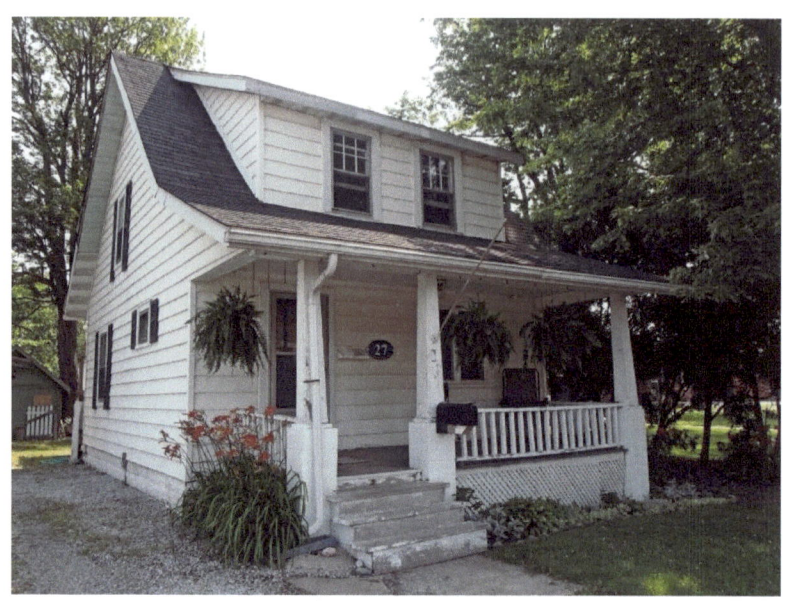

27 Talbot Street South

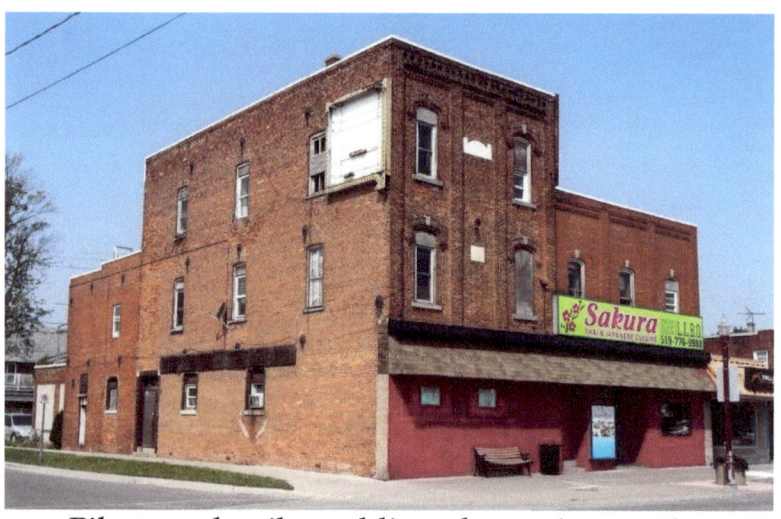

Pilasters, dentil moulding, decorative cornice

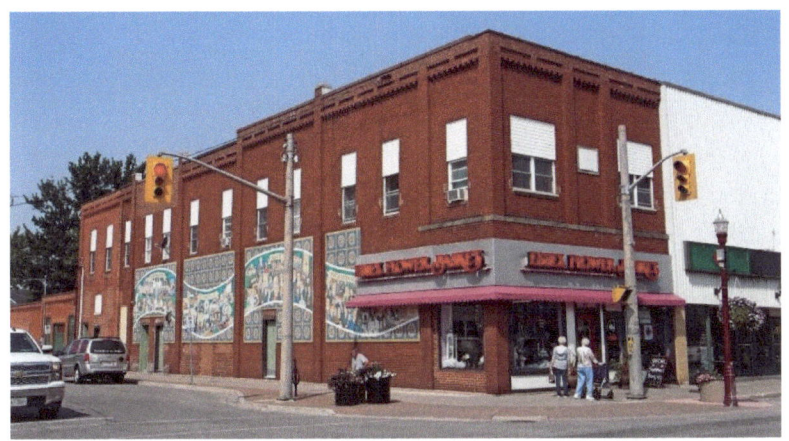

Talbot Street South – dentil moulding

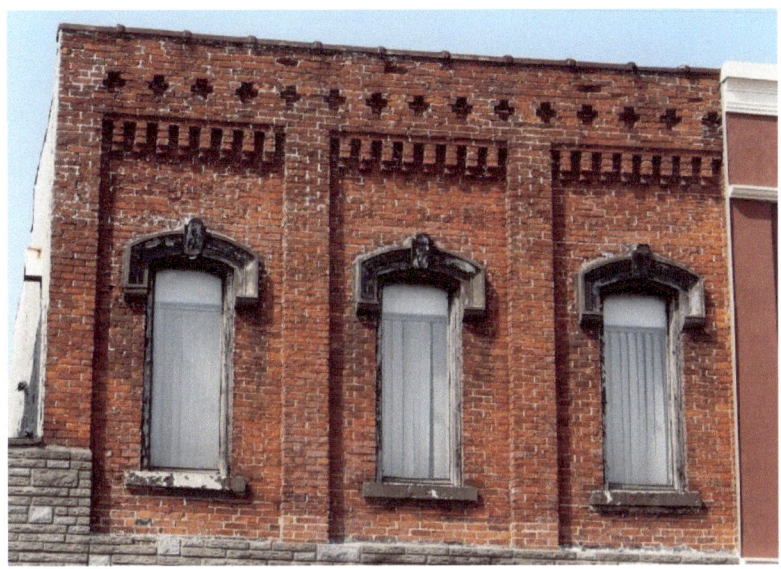

Talbot Street South – window hoods, bevelled dentil
moulding, decorative brickwork, pilasters

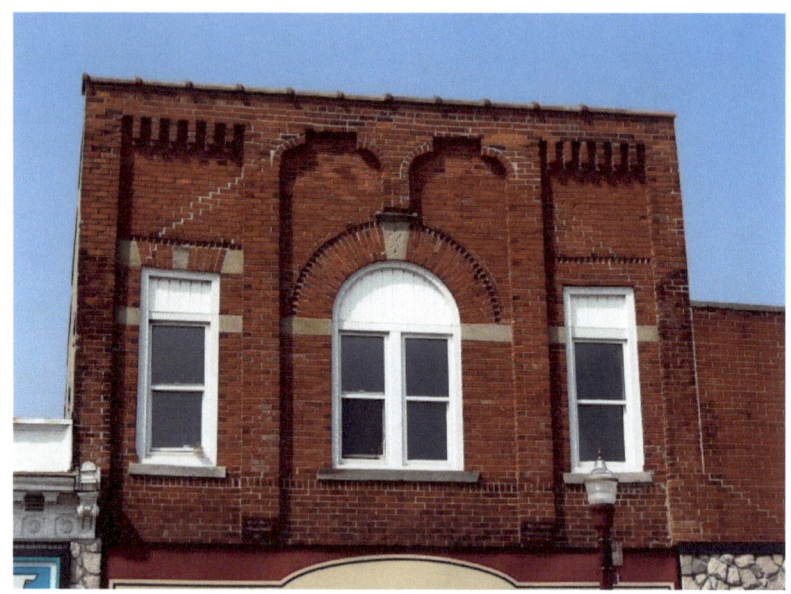

Talbot Street South – bevelled dentil moulding, arched voussoir with keystone, pilasters

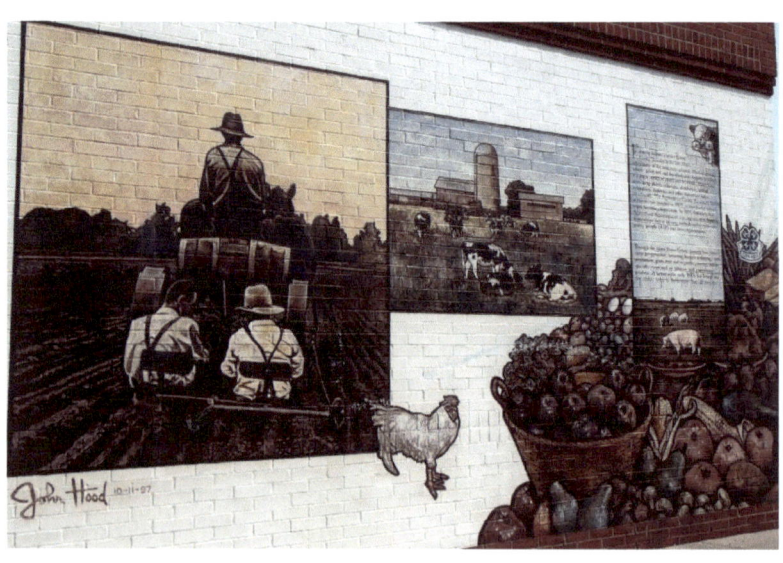

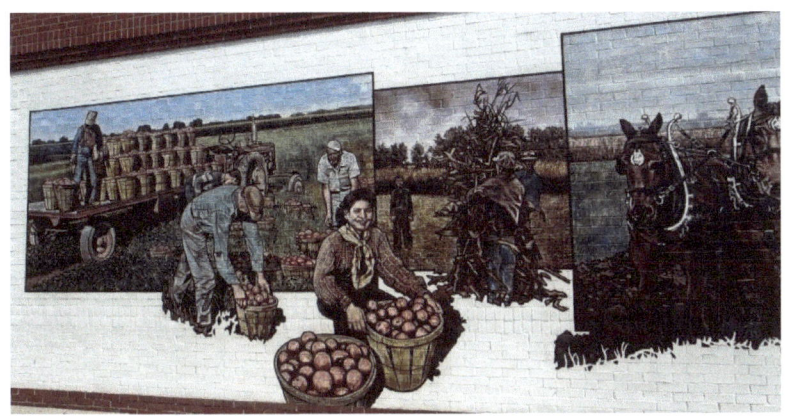

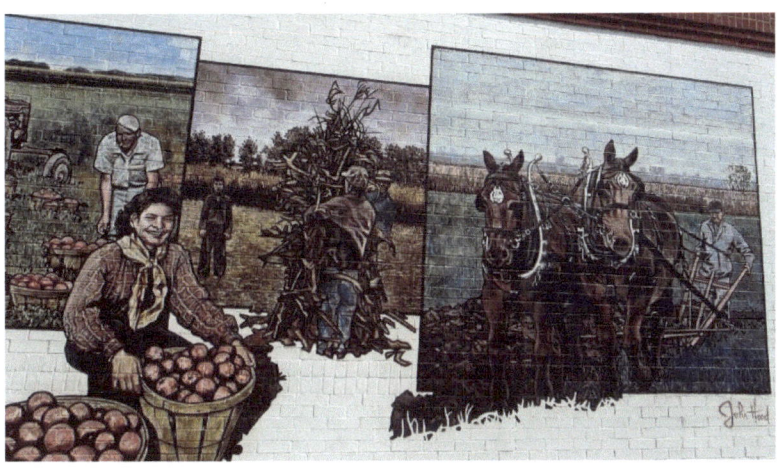

Farming was a major Essex County industry in the late 1800s when many of the trees were cleared. The long growing season, good soil, and knowledgeable farmers resulted in a great variety of crops and livestock. Many food processing plants, wineries, distilleries, milling companies, bakeries and other industries were developed. Through the years Essex County have been leaders in dairying, pork production, grain, fruit and vegetable growing, and in specialty crops such as tobacco and greenhouse produce. A farmer in the early 1900s fed himself and 5 others; today, a farmer feeds more than 125 people.

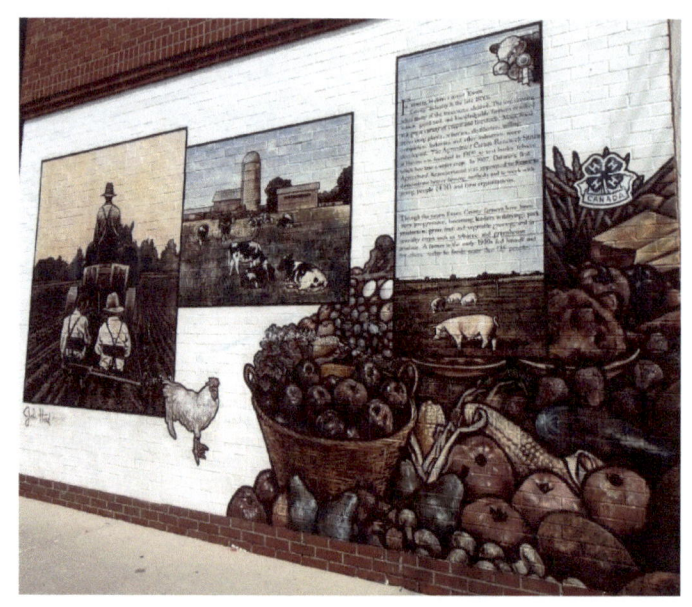

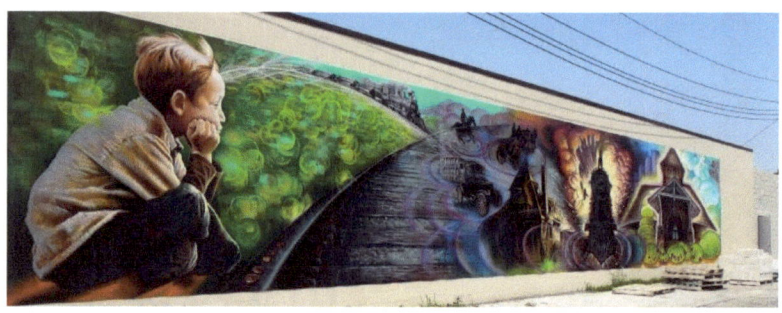

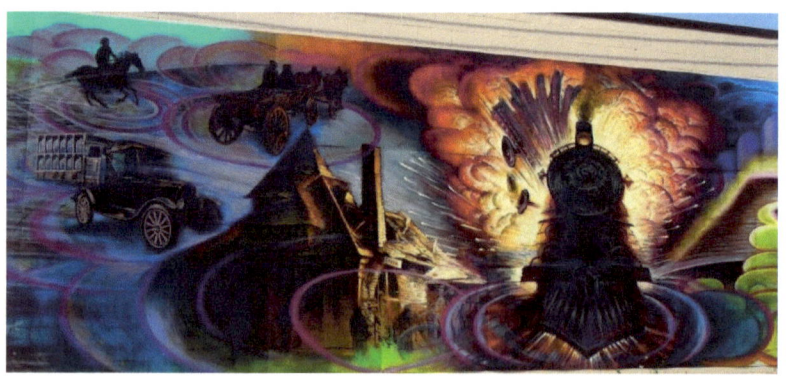

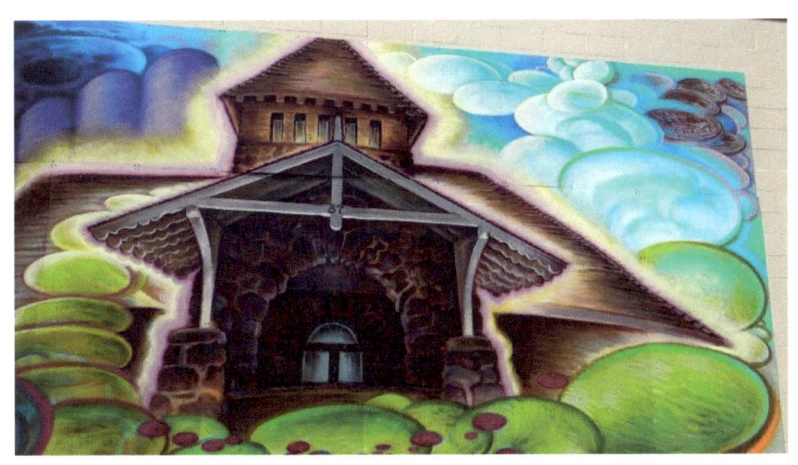

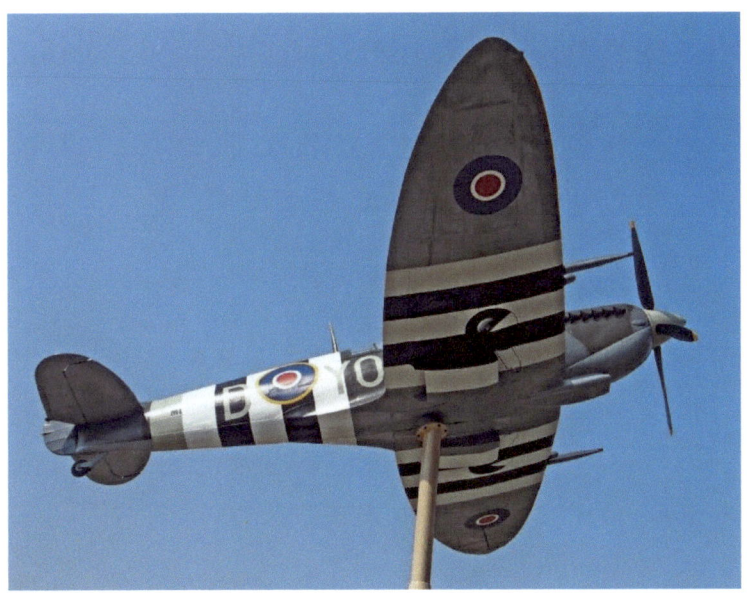

Essex Memorial Spitfire

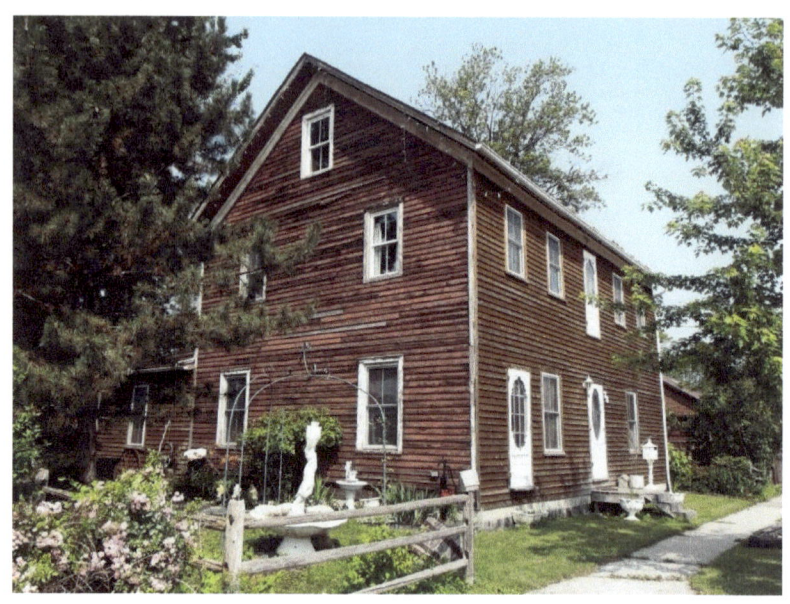

78 Fox Street – Gothic/Georgian style – wooden building

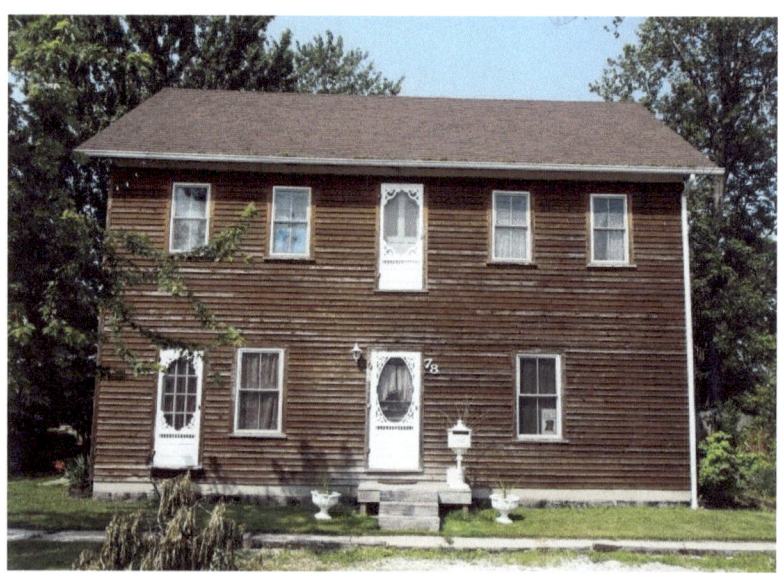

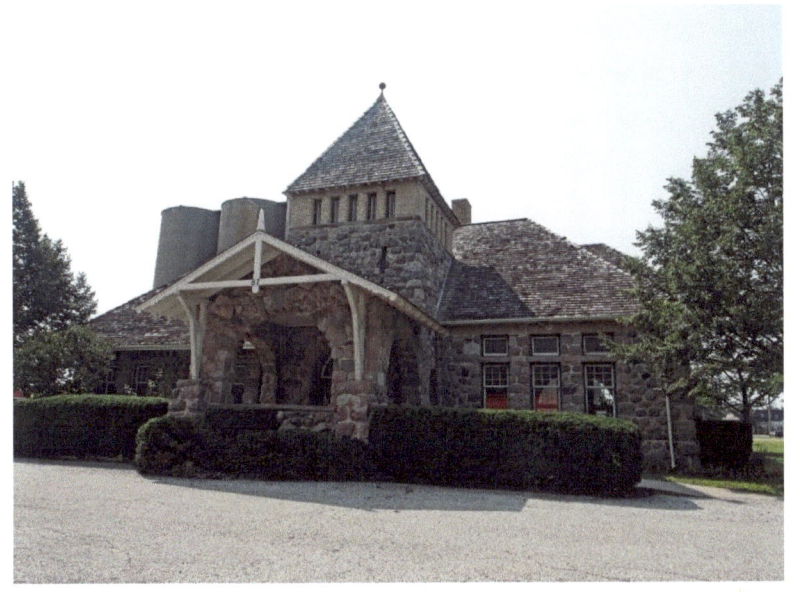

Essex Railway Station – cobblestone train station - 1887

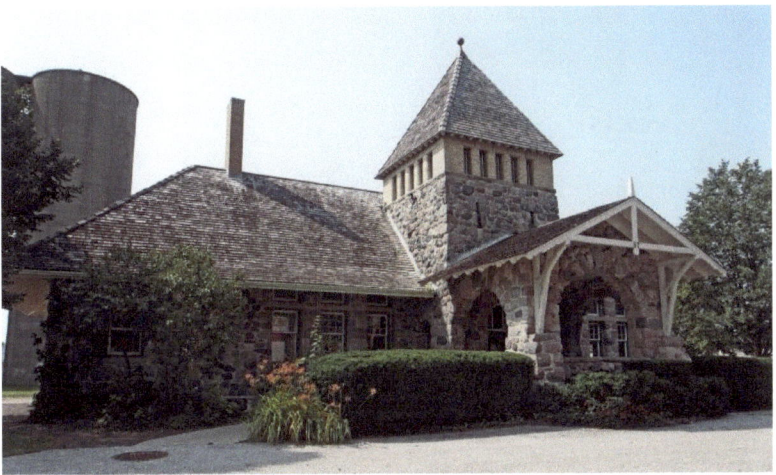

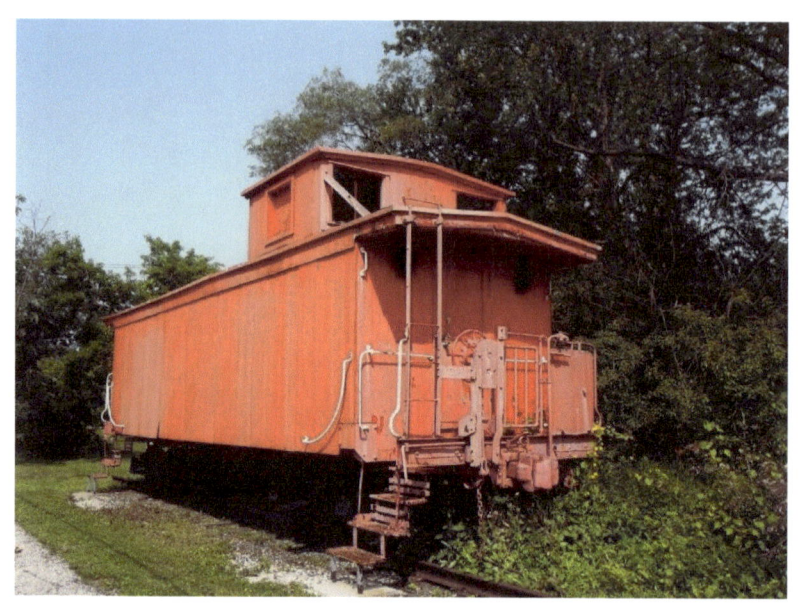

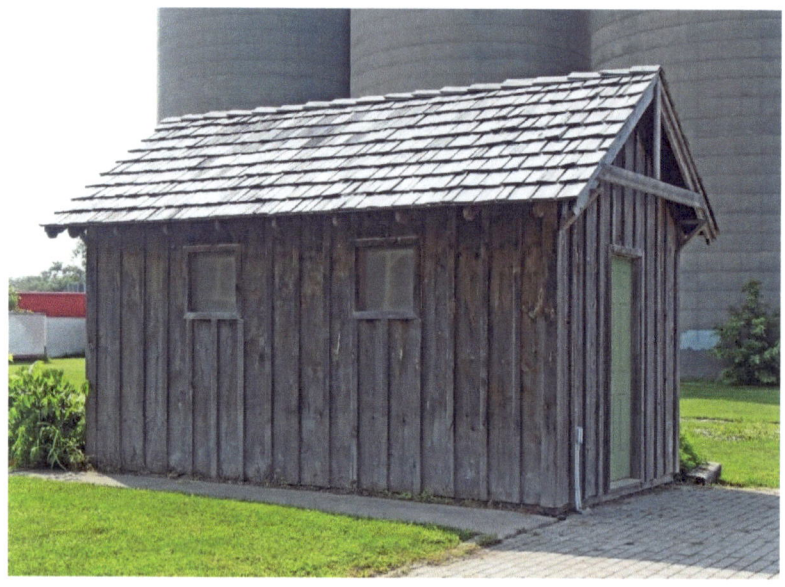

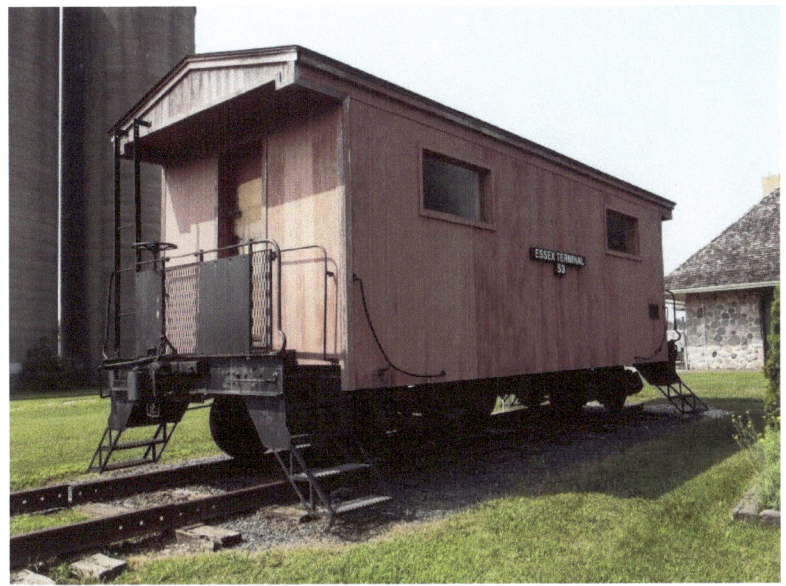

Essex Terminal Railway Caboose #53 – a unique car that was one of two cars built about 1909 – sits on arch bar trucks from steam locomotive tenders (these trucks were banned in the 1920s and the car was limited to use on Essex Terminal Railway tracks).

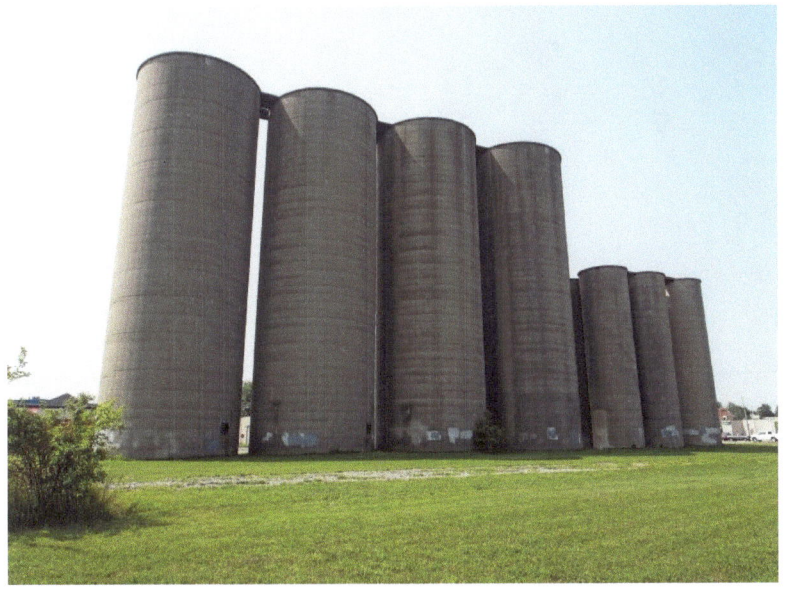

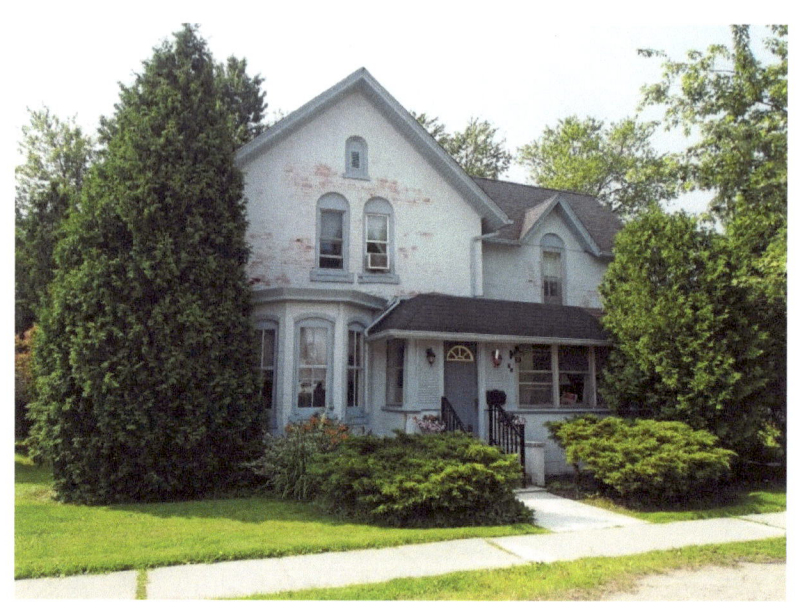

56 Cameron Avenue – Gothic Revival

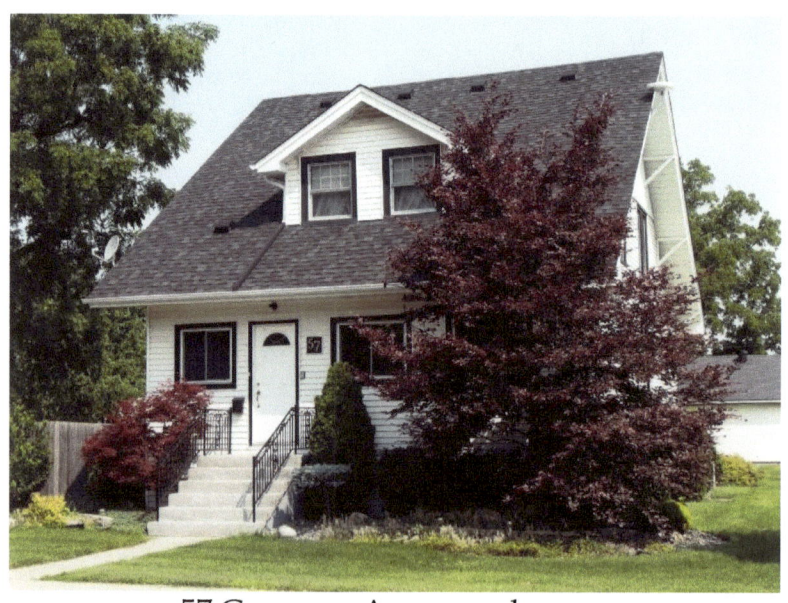

57 Cameron Avenue - dormer

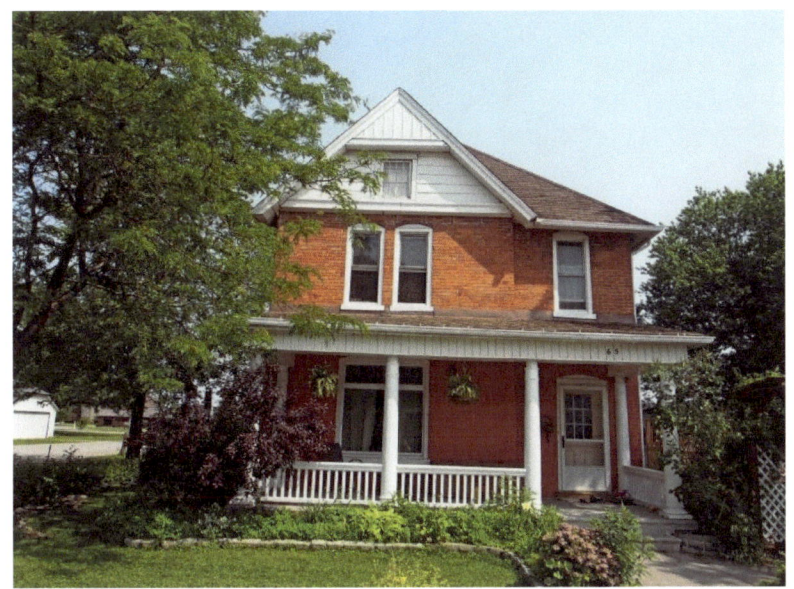

65 Cameron Avenue – Edwardian

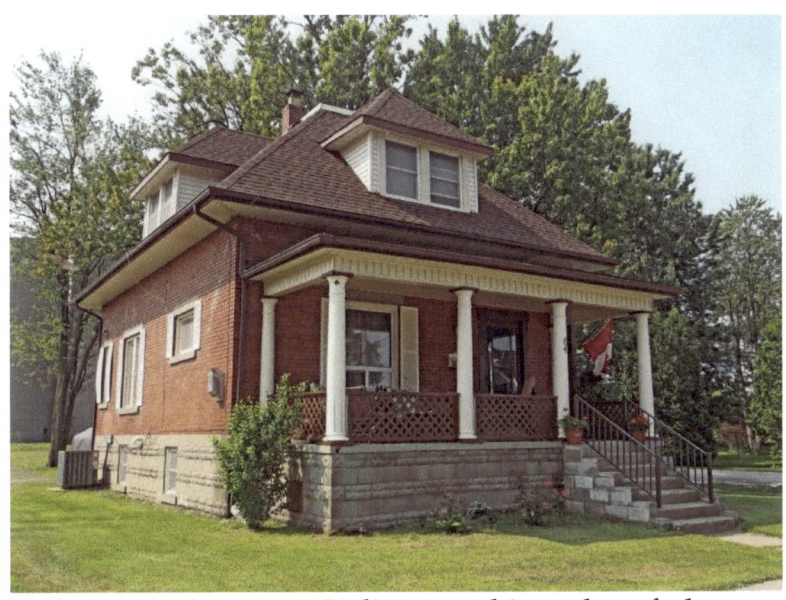

64 Cameron Avenue – Italianate – hipped roof, dormers

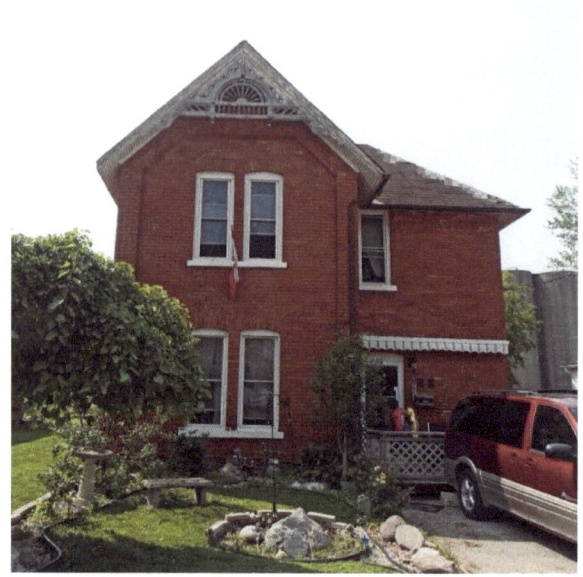

72 Cameron Avenue – Gothic Revival, verge board trim on gable with spindles and stenciling

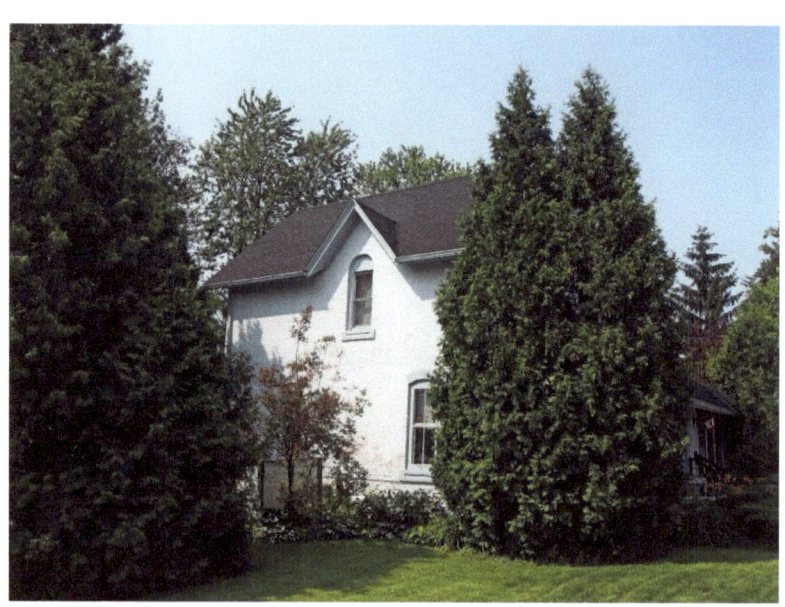

56 Cameron Avenue – Gothic Revival

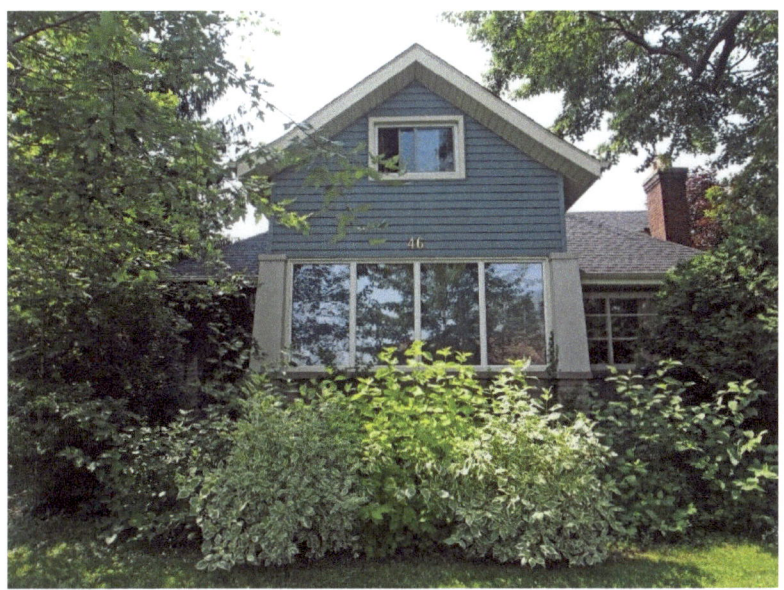

46 Cameron Avenue

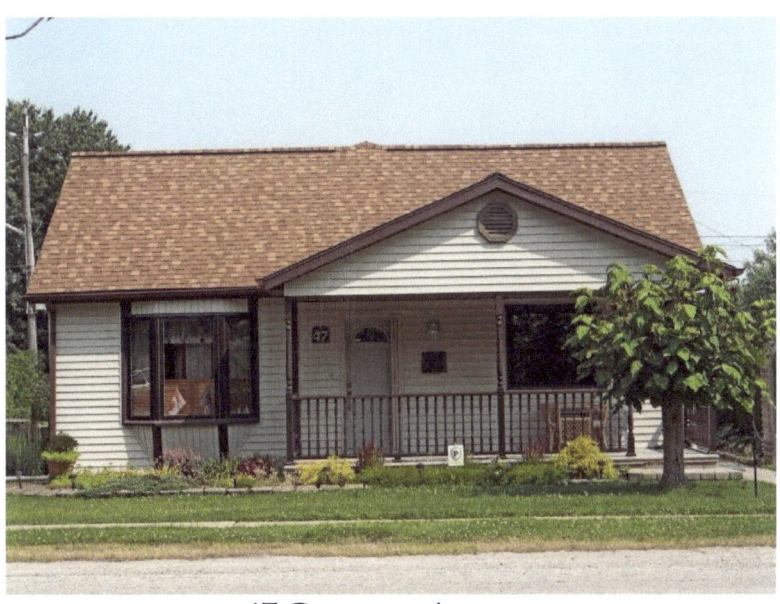

47 Cameron Avenue

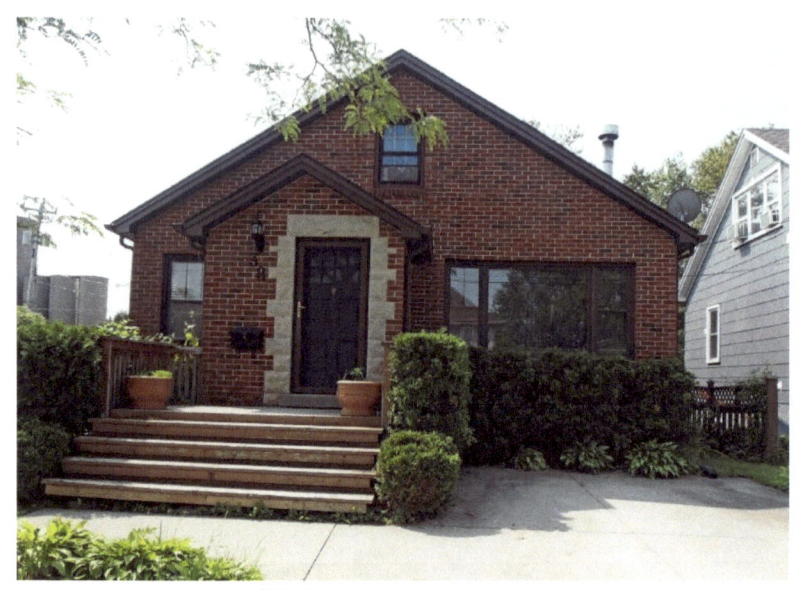

38 Cameron Avenue

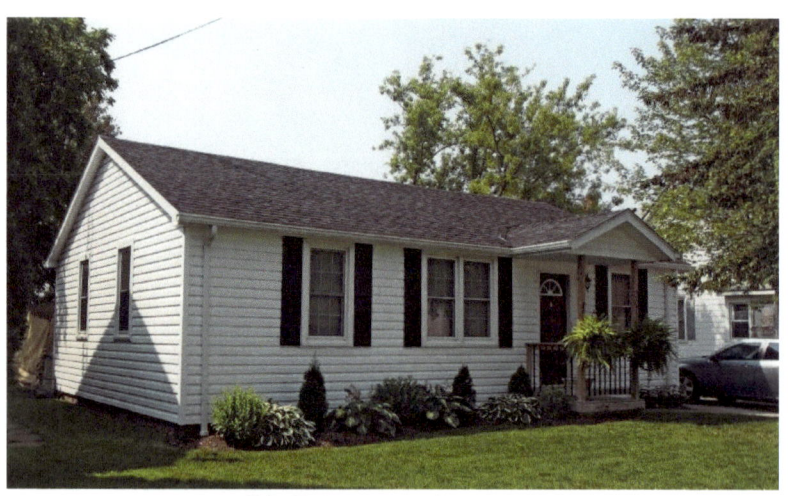

30 Cameron Avenue

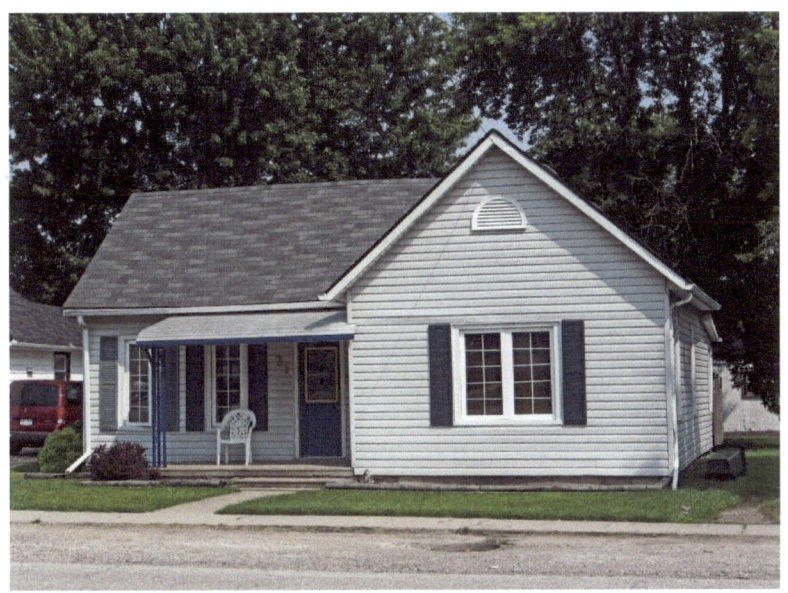

31 Cameron Avenue

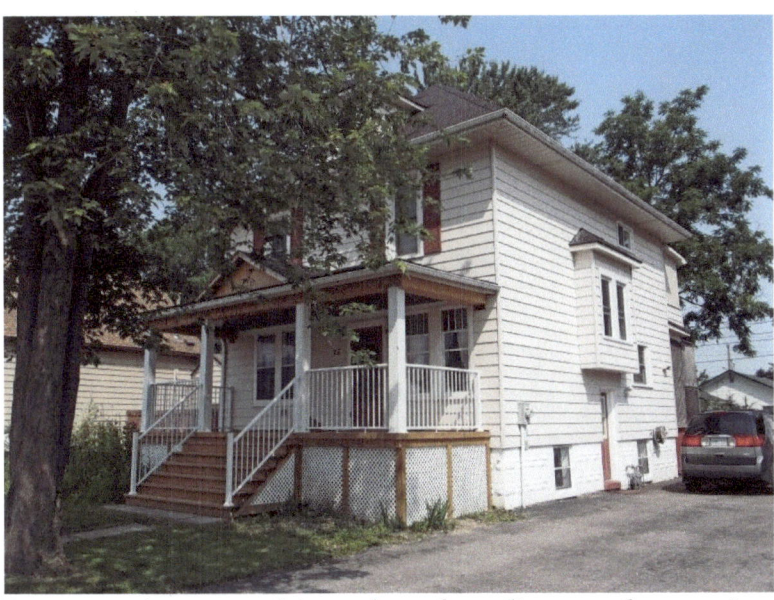

23 Cameron Avenue – hipped roof, pediment, dormer in attic

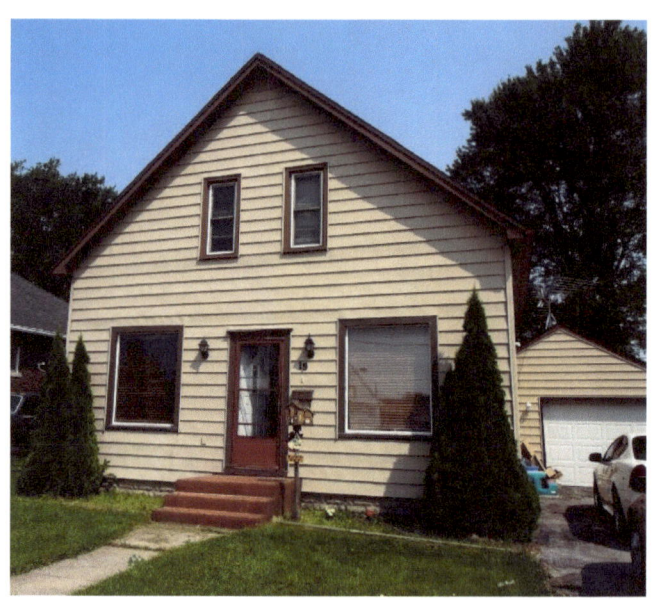

19 Cameron Avenue

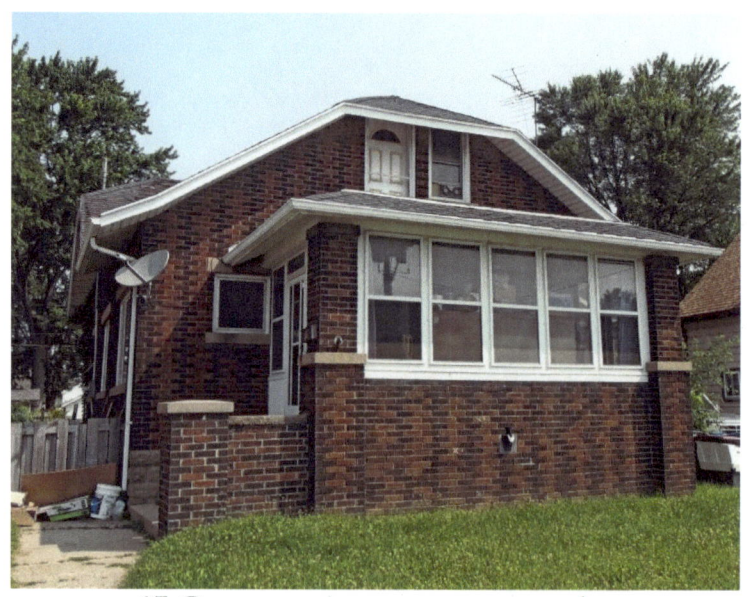

15 Cameron Avenue – vernacular

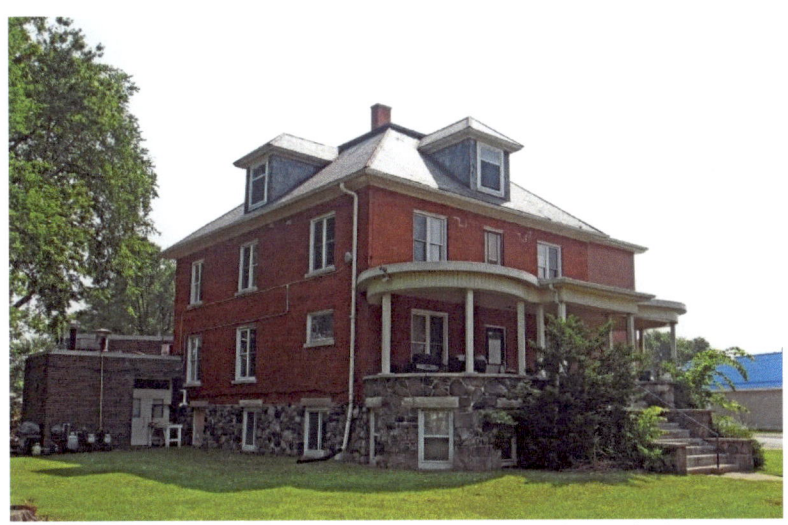

Talbot Street North – Italianate, hipped roof, dormers, cobblestone basement walls

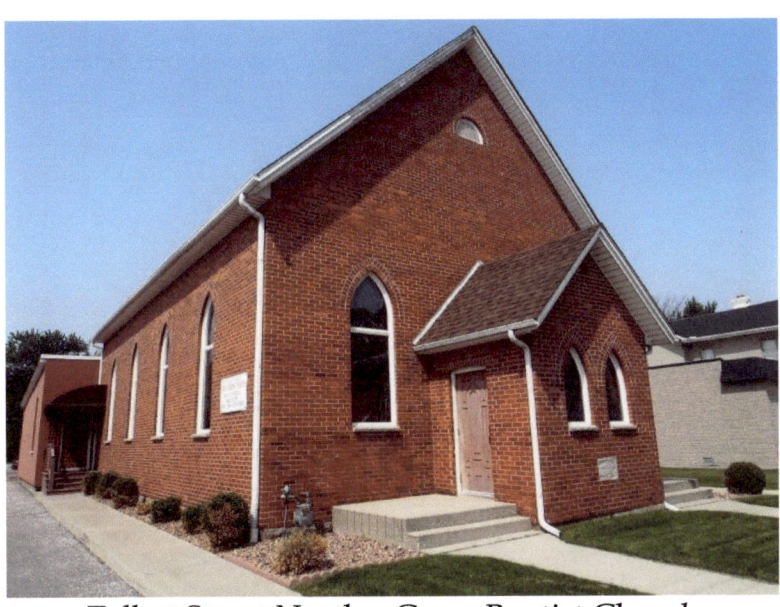

Talbot Street North – Grace Baptist Church

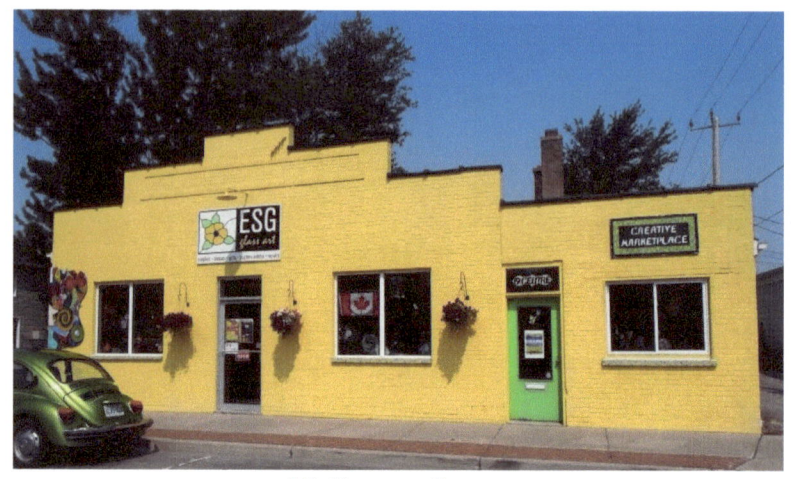

19 Centre Street

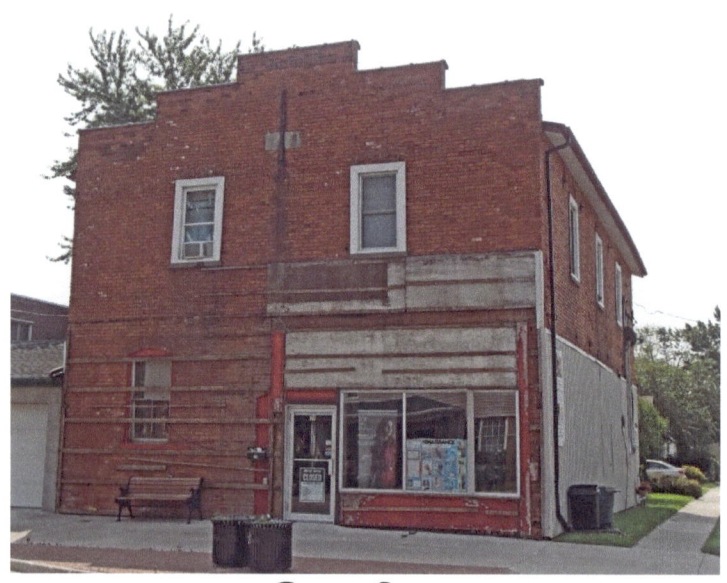

Centre Street

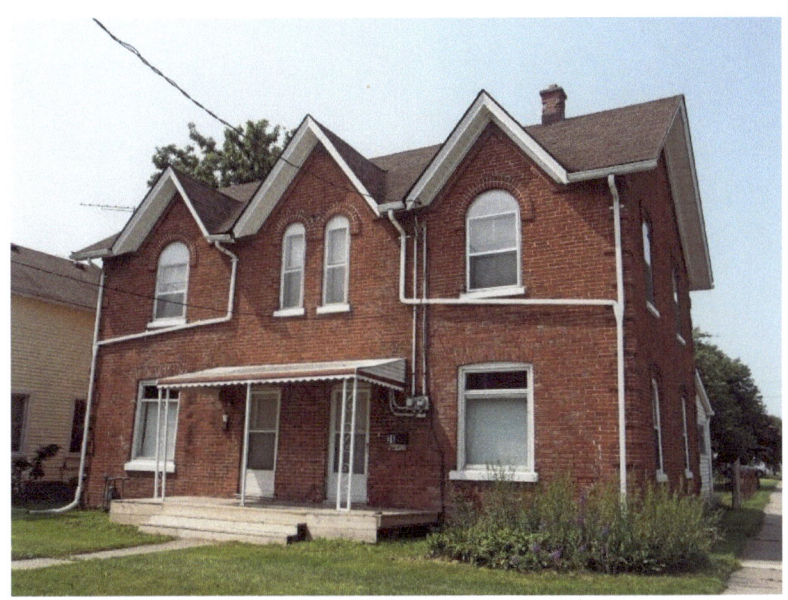

36 Centre Street – triple-gable Gothic Revival

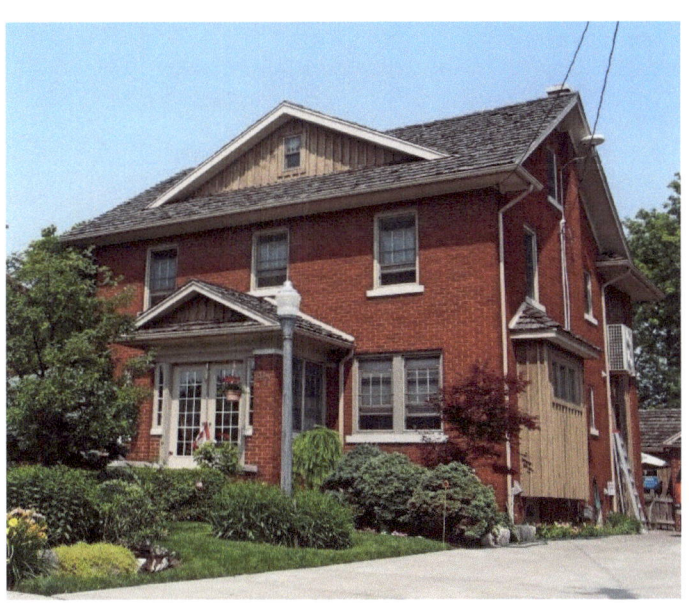

Centre Street

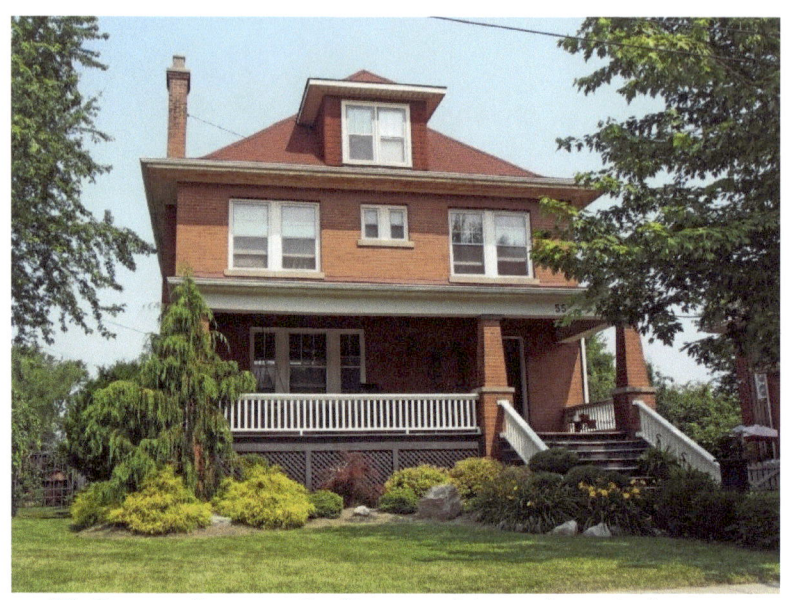

55 Centre Street – Italianate, hipped roof, dormer

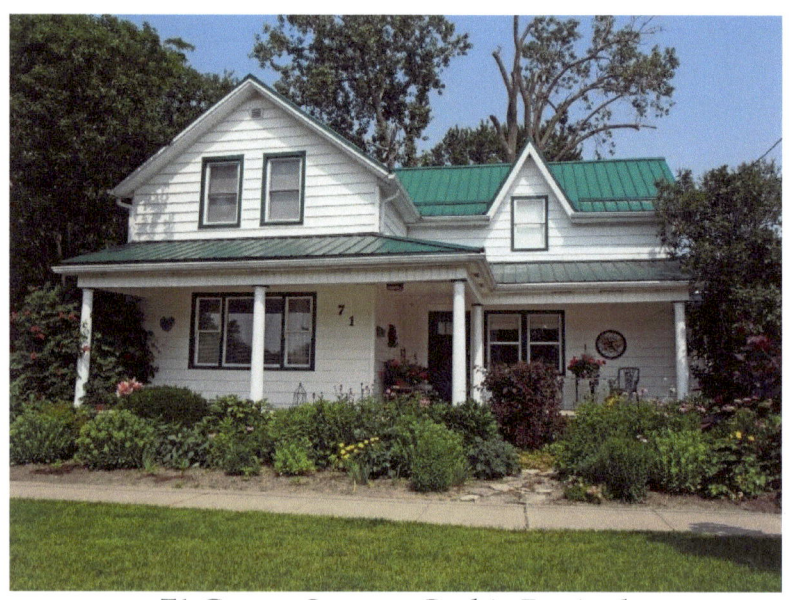

71 Centre Street – Gothic Revival

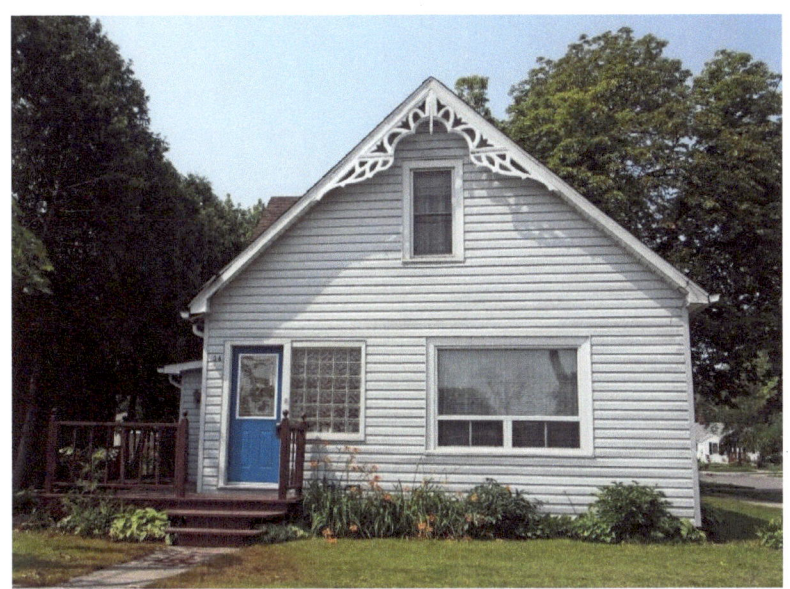

34 Centre Street – verge board trim on gable

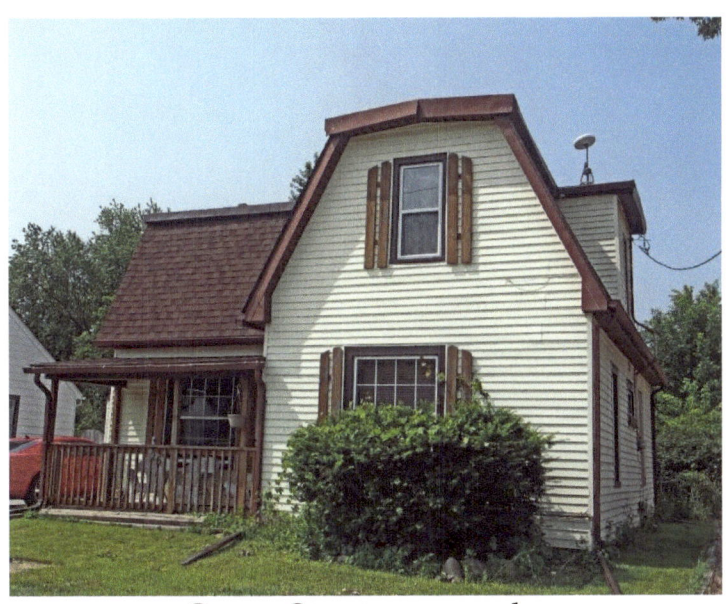

Centre Street - vernacular

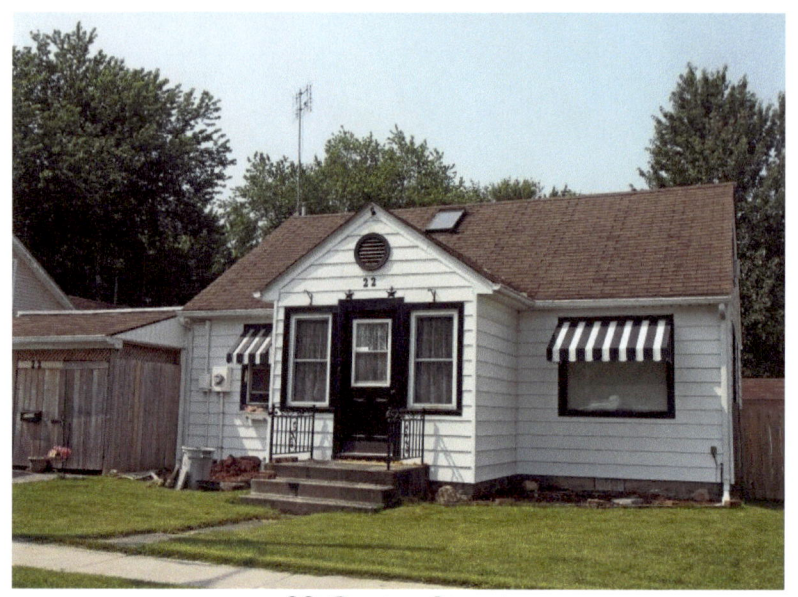

22 Centre Street

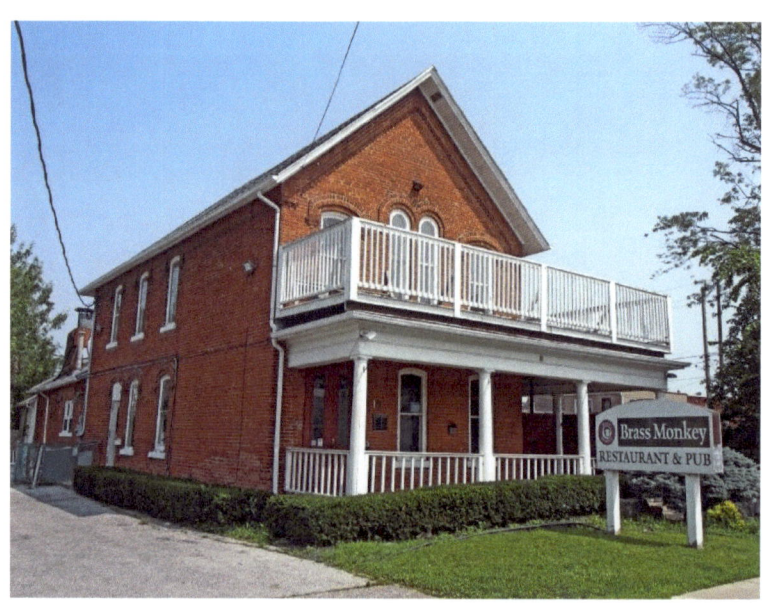

19 Laird Avenue – Brass Monkey Restaurant and Pub
Gothic Revival

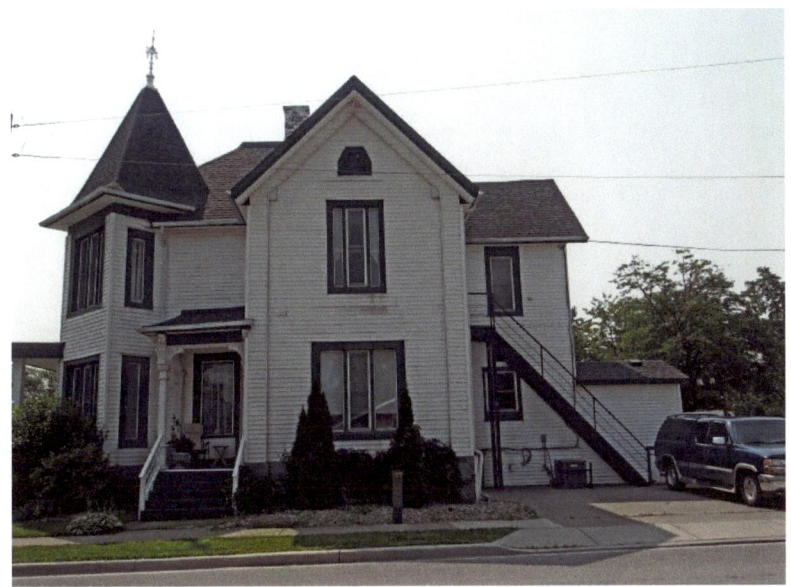

122 Talbot Street South – Essex Manor Rest Home
Two-storey, Queen Anne style

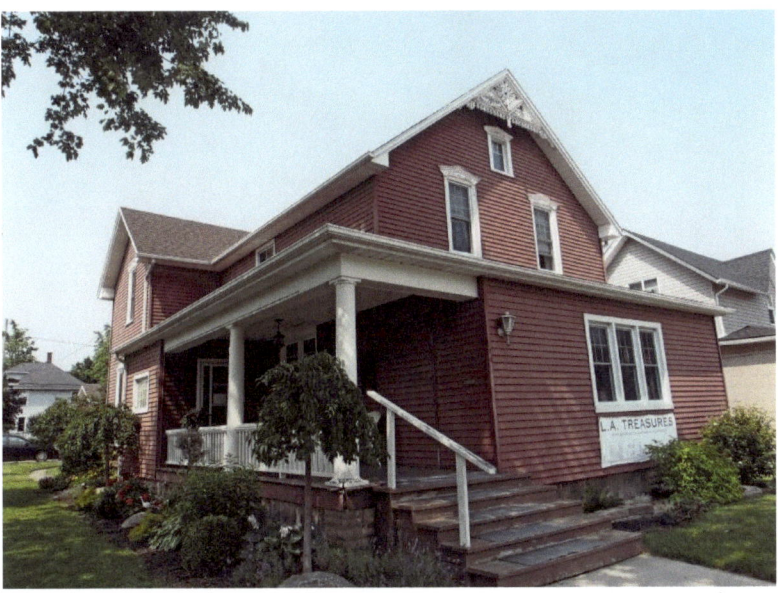

Talbot Street South – gable decoration with stenciling

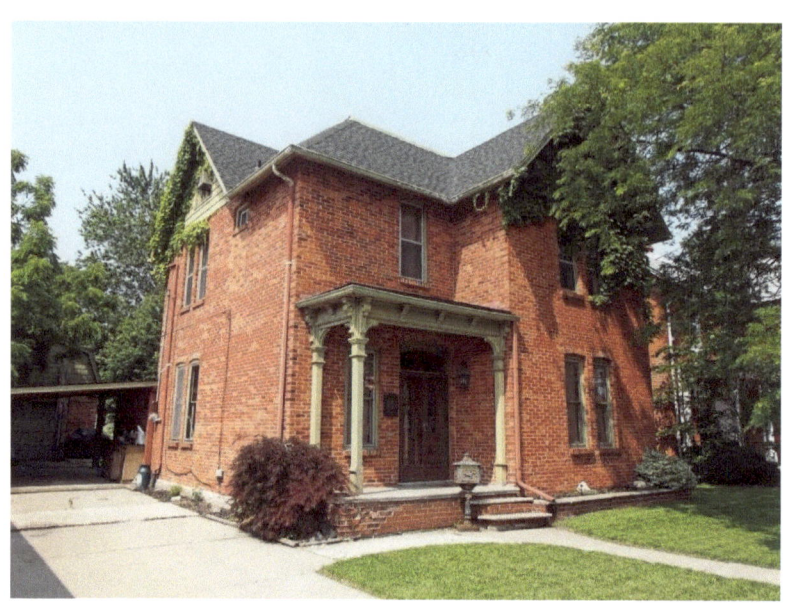

102 Talbot Street South – Gothic Revival

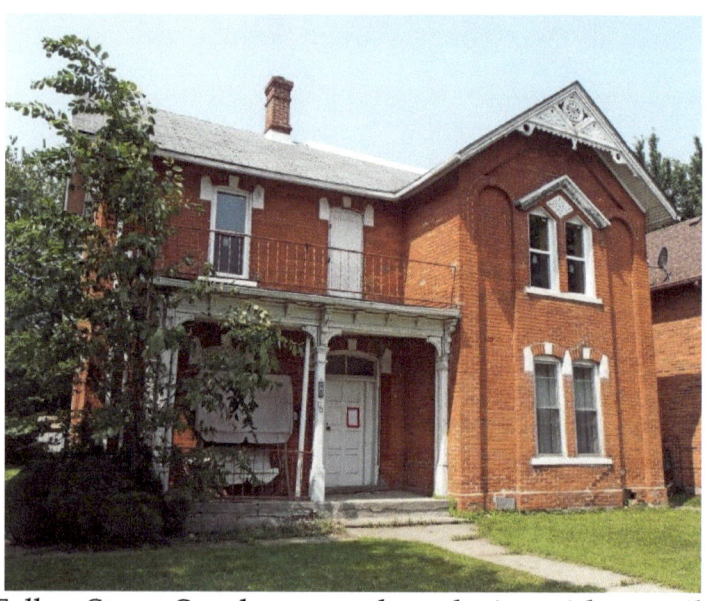

98 Talbot Street South – verge board trim with stenciling,
stenciling above second-floor window, second floor balcony

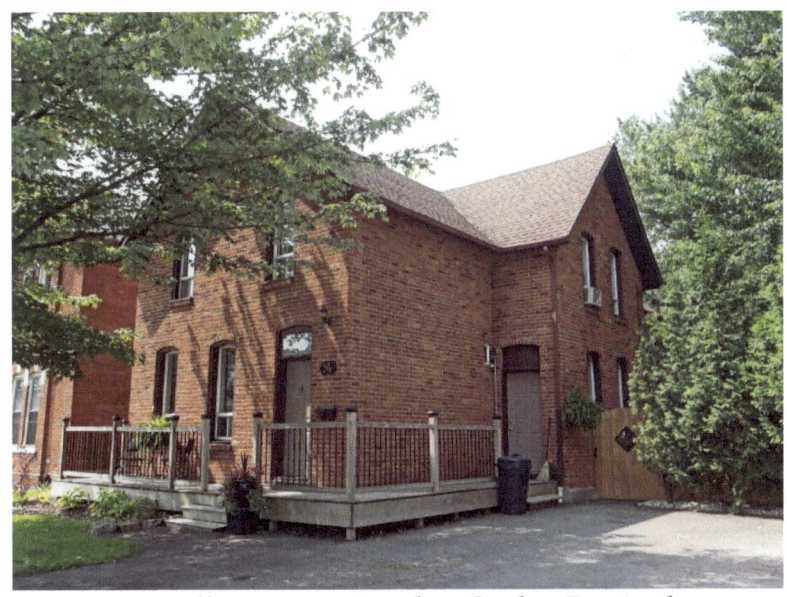

94 Talbot Street South – Gothic Revival

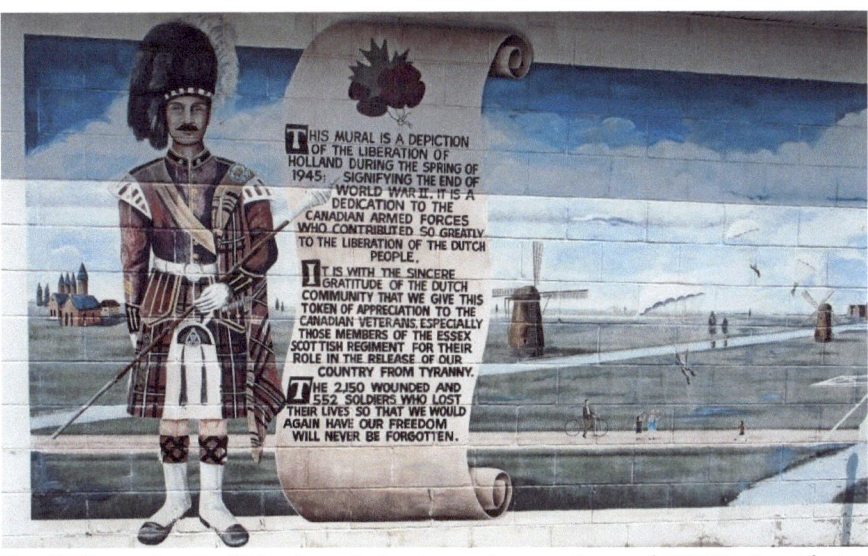

The Liberation of Holland during the spring of 1945 signifying
the end of World War II

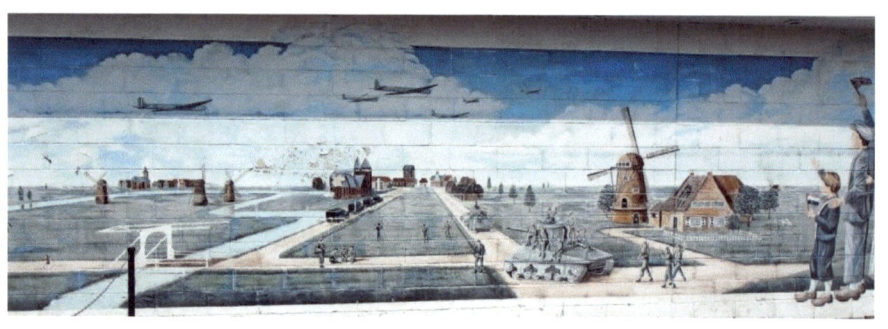

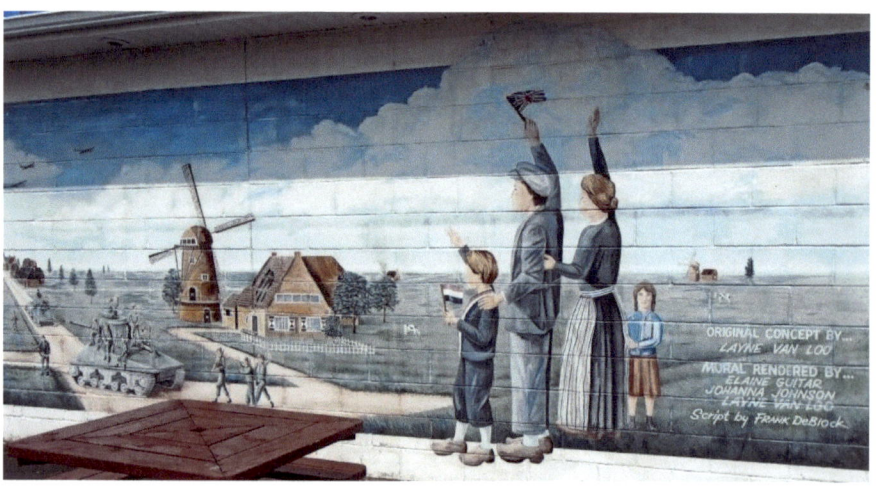

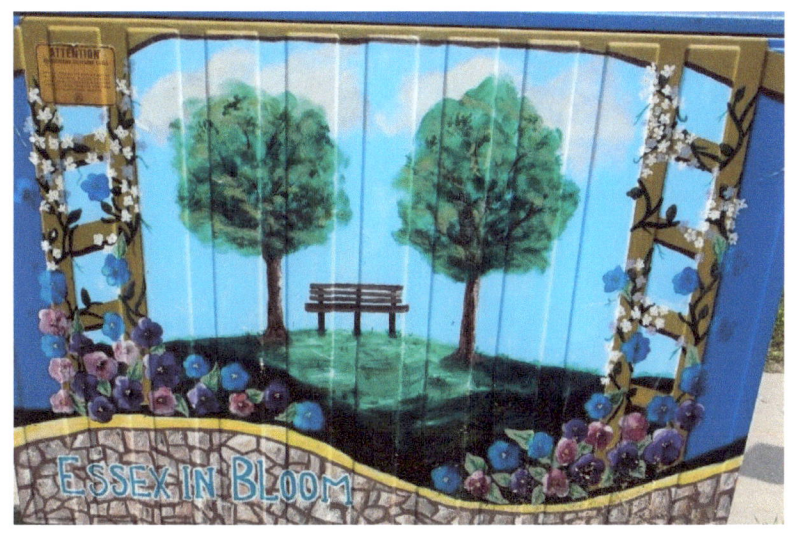

Essex in Bloom mural

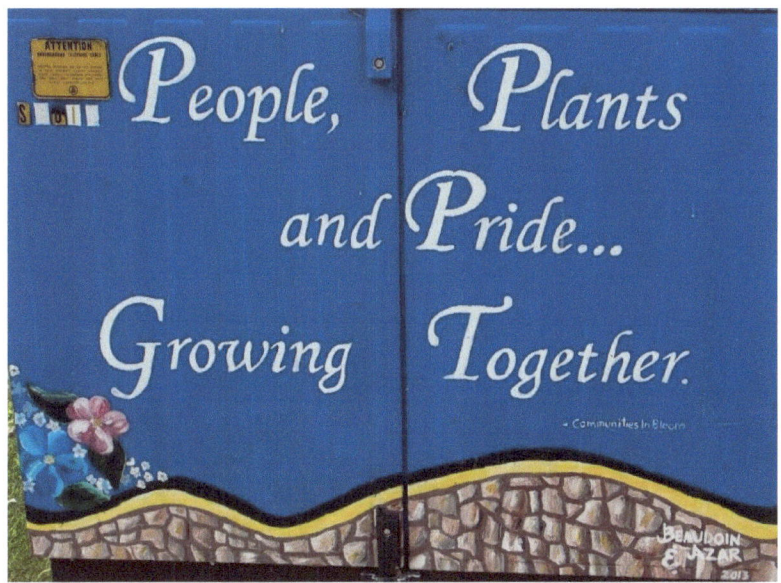

Bay Window: A window that projects out from a wall, in a semicircular, rectangular, or polygonal design. Used frequently in Gothic and Victorian designs. Example: 54 Talbot Street South, Page 22	
Brackets: a decorative or weight-bearing structural element which forms a right angle with one side against a wall and the other under a projecting surface such as an eave or roof. Example: 54 Talbot Street South, Page 22	
Cobblestone architecture: Refers to the use of cobblestones embedded in mortar as a method for erecting walls on houses and commercial buildings. Example: Essex Railway Station, Page 37	
Cornice: originally the wooden overhang of the roof. With the use of stone, brick, iron and steel, the cornice is any projecting shelf at the top of a ceiling or roof. They can be very decorative. Example: Page 10	
Dentil Moulding: an even series of rectangles used as ornamental decoration in cornices. Example: Page 32	

Dormer: (French for "sleep") a gable end window that pierces through the plane of a sloping roof surface to create usable space in the top floor or attic of a building by adding headroom. Example: 64 Cameron Avenue, Page 41	
Gable: the triangular portion of a wall between the edges of a sloping roof. Example: 72 Cameron Avenue, Page 42	
Hipped Roof: a roof where all sides slope downwards to the walls with no gables. Example: Talbot Street North, Page 47	
Keystones and Voussoirs: a voussoir is a wedge-shaped element used in building an arch. A keystone is the central stone that locks all the stones into position, allowing the arch to bear weight. A keystone is often enlarged and embellished. Example: Page 10	
Lancet Window: a tall, narrow window with a pointed arch at its top. Example: Talbot Street North - Grace Baptist Church, Page 47	

Pediment: a triangular section above the horizontal structure (entablature), typically supported by columns. The inside of the triangle is called the tympanum. Example: 23 Cameron Avenue, Page 45	
Pilaster: a slightly projecting column built into or applied to the face of a wall for additional structural support. Example:	
Turret: a small tower that projects from the wall of a building. Example: 122 Talbot Street South, Page 53	
Vergeboard and Finial: also called bargeboards – hang from the projecting end of a roof and are often elaborately carved and ornamented. **Finial:** ornament added to the top of a gable, pinnacle, canopy or spire – a Gothic element. Example: 72 Cameron Avenue, Page 42	
Window Hood: A **hood** is the piece found above window openings, usually of an ornate design, and covers the top third of the opening. Hoods are commonly placed above arched or curved openings on both windows and doors. Example: Talbot Street South, Page 31	

Building Styles

Arts and Crafts: The overlying theme - the house was based on the function of the house. Rooms were oriented to take advantage of the movement of the sun for warmth and light during daylight hours. Side entrances allowed for useable space on the front facade for light or garden use. Arts and Crafts houses have many of these features: wood, stone or stucco siding; low-pitched roof; wide eaves with triangular brackets; exposed roof rafters; porch with thick square or round columns; stone porch supports; exterior chimney made with stone; open floor plans with few hallways; many windows, some with stained or leaded glass; beamed ceilings; dark wood wainscoting and moldings; built-in cabinets, shelves, and seating. Example: Essex Railway Station, Page 37	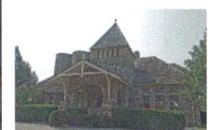
Cape Dutch architecture is a traditional Afrikaner architectural style found mostly in the Western Cape of South Africa. The initial settlers of the Cape were primarily Dutch. When the Dutch came to Ontario, they brought with them building concepts from their own native lands. Architecture from the 18th and early 19th centuries in Ontario includes a wide assortment of detailing and ornament all applied to a basic building design centred around the fireplace and the source of water. Example: 80 Irwin Avenue, Page 17	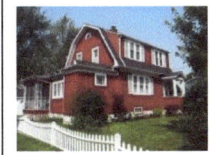

Edwardian, 1900-1930 – This style bridges the ornate and elaborate styles of the Victorian era and the simplified styles of the 20th century. Balanced facades, simple roof lines, dormer windows, large front porches, and smooth brick surfaces are its characteristics. Example: 65 Cameron Avenue, Page 41	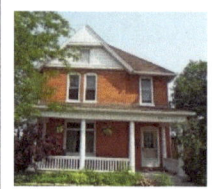
Georgian, before 1860 – This style began with the British King Georges in the 18th century. These buildings have balanced facades around a central door, medium-pitched gable roofs, and small paned windows. Example: 78 Fox Street, Page 36	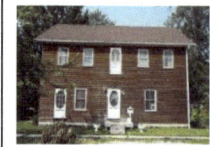
Gothic Revival, 1830-1890 – These decorative buildings have sharply-pitched gables with highly detailed verge boards, pointed-arch window openings, and dichromatic brickwork. It is a common style in Ontario. Example: 36 Centre Street, Page 49	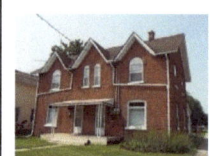
Italianate, 1850-1900 – It has wide-bracketed eaves, belvederes, wrap-around verandahs. Example: 55 Centre Street, Page 50	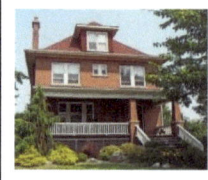

Queen Anne, 1885-1900 – This style is distinguished by an irregular outline featuring a combination of an offset tower, broad gables, projecting two-storey bays, verandahs, multi-sloped roofs, and tall, decorative chimneys. A mixture of brick and wood is common. Windows often have one large single-paned bottom sash and small panes in the upper sash. Example: 122 Talbot Street South, Page 53	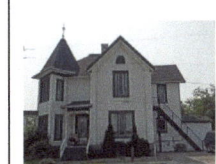
Vernacular/Traditional Mode 1638 - 1950 Influenced but not defined by a particular style, vernacular buildings are made from easily available materials and exhibit local design characteristics. Example: 46 Alice Street, Page 27	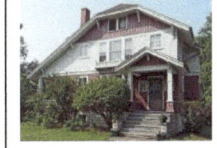

www.ingramcontent.com/pod-product-compliance
Lightning Source LLC
Chambersburg PA
CBHW041106180526
45172CB00001B/130